Ronald Duncan
Collected Poems

Other Works by Ronald Duncan

POETRY

Postcards to Pulcinella
The Mongrel
The Solitudes
Man (Parts I–V)

Judas
Unpopular Poems
For the Few
Selected Poems

PLAYS

The Dull Ass's Hoof
This Way to the Tomb
Stratton
The Rape of Lucretia
Don Juan
Our Lady's Tumbler

The Death of Satan
Abelard and Héloïse
The Catalyst
O.B.A.F.G
Selected Plays

PROSE

Journal of a Husbandman
Home-Made Home
Tobacco Growing in England
The Blue Fox
Jan's Journal

Saint Spiv
The Perfect Mistress
The Kettle of Fish
The Tale of Tails
The Last Adam

ADAPTATIONS

The Eagle has Two Heads
The Typewriter
The Apollo de Bellac

The Rabbit Race
Beauty and the Beast
The Trojan Women

EDITIONS

The Selected Writings of
    Mahatma Gandhi
Selected Lyrics and Satires of
    the Earl of Rochester

The Poems of Ben Jonson
Dante: De Vulgari Eloquentia
The Encyclopaedia of
    Ignorance

AUTOBIOGRAPHY

All Men are Islands
Obsessed

How to Make Enemies

Ronald Duncan
Collected Poems

Collected and edited
by
Miranda Weston-Smith

Heinemann
Quixote Press

Heinemann/Quixote Press
10 Upper Grosvenor Street, London W1X 9PA

LONDON MELBOURNE TORONTO
JOHANNESBURG AUCKLAND

First published 1981
© Ronald Duncan
SBN 434 98022 6

Printed and bound in Great Britain by
Fletcher & Son Ltd, Norwich

Contents

Introduction	xxi
Editorial Note	xxiii

1928
'Huge cliffs shoulder the sea. You can' (Danse Macabre)†	1

1929
'It is of woman's love I sing' (Canzone: The River)	3

1931
'Life's easy for her' (Tempusque Virgo)	4

1933
'When men hunger and women' (Had we the time)	5
'I can remember my Mother's womb' (For Continuity)	6
'Who really loves me?'	6
'It was as if I'd met the Lord,' (Confessio Amantis)	7

1934
'Because I enjoy a solitary tree' (Aria)	8

1935
'The earth's excited with leaf and labour'	9
'I turned in time to see a star, stretch' (Insignificance)	11
'When may I introduce to you' (Mr Holy Ghost)	11
'The Blessed Sacrament said here' (Parish Church)	12

† Titles of poems are given in brackets, ed.

1936

'Do what Rimbaud did – eh?' (Question)	14
'Not in the swing of the year' (Poem)	15
'It is essential that an ultimatum should be sent' (After dinner speech)	15
'Knowing that a cock or a bull' (Epigram)	16
'Night like a lean leopard' (The Panther)	17
'Passion's no Prince'	17

1937

'The maddening traffic of my dreams' (Poet 1937)	19
'Were the curls' (Jou-Jou)	20
'Spring is no certain thing'	20
'Across the desert'	21
'Let's speak around and about yesterday,'	21
'Oh earth, I am in love with thee' (Song of the Earth)	22

1938

'Give me your hand' (Our difficulty is)	23
'I worry how to tell my love'	24
'The revolving Earth' (Plain Song)	24
'I wonder if her wise, wide eyes'	25
'Sooner or later, you' (Song)	26
'The clean shy leaves undress the trees' (Song)	26

1939

'Her birthday, – up she gets, she's twenty-three;' (Unfinished Eulogy)	28
'For an old reason' (Phallic Song, I)	29
'The girl at the factory took me in,' (Looney's Song)	30

1940

'Today the Vicar came down – it being Good Friday' (Postcard)	31
'Night creeps'	32
'Strong as the Nelson Column and with no pigeons on it;' (Phallic Song, II)	32
'Veins can, as vines climb, swell,' (Experiment with old Metaphors)	33
'Isn't there something in common' (Song to Sea)	33
'Sheaves of grass,' (Hayharvest song)	34

1941

'Let us start here: for this, is where we are.' (Feast of Sowing) — 35

1942

'Love like a dog barks' (Canzone) — 36
'Noticing that one of our randy guns' (Poems from the War, I) — 41
'Ah well! All these sailors' (Poems from the War, II) — 42
'I who had sound health and a wife' (The Miller's Lament) — 42
'Spring's first enthusiasm fades' — 47
'Husband!' (Spanish Song) — 47

1943

'In a six-cylinder fury' (Poem) — 48
'Oh my God with what agility' (Solitude, 1) — 49
'At the thrust of the stiff Spring, oh la,' (Dansa) — 50
'Oh Rose Marie as you are my love' (Aubade) — 51
'Great Souls in prison cells' (Ballad of Stratton Gaol) — 55
'What is Summer' (Summer) — 57
'Jasmine lies as gently on the evening air' — 57
'I am kneeling in the chapel of Saint Simon,' (Song) — 58

1944

'At Windsor where the castle keep' (For a young man, aged 90) — 59
'Oh, I wish I were an orange tree,' (The Crone's Lament) — 61
'Like skulls with all their fears still there' (Air Raid) — 62
'With the vision of the blind' (Strophe and Anti-Strophe at Bakerloo) — 63
'My heart burns away slowly' (Mi Pensamiento) — 64
'He was neither prince nor politician' (The Mason's Epitaph) — 65
'Christ, is this thy Cross, tossed?' (Flotsam) — 67
'Where waves of earth' (Dartmoor) — 67
'Does the terror of the tiger's tooth' (The Mongrel) — 68

1945

'They say that man is blessed with sight' (The Single Eye) — 78
'Like little clouds on a green sky, my sheep' (Impromptu for a child) — 79

'Like a waterfall of wind' (Briony)	79
'And this evening as the sun' (Moto Perpetuo)	81
'The Site: choose a dry site' (Practical Ballad, I)	82
'Some people don't like the rain. I like the rain' (Practical Ballad, II)	83
'In a blind world of grass' (To Plough)	83
'The thick blood of my heart' (Notes of a dream)	84
'Old bottles on an old shelf contain' (Lines written for a Wine Merchant's Christmas card)	85
'This song's to a girl' (Carol)	85

1946

'Oh my love, I am as lonely' (Appenato)	87
'Drink! For the night is flowing like black wine,' (Drinking Song)	88

1947

'It was not that I raised myself to Him' (Ascension)	89

1948

'Having descended the escalator at Queensway Tube Station' (Epitaph on an unknown passenger)	91

1949

'To her whose eyes are eloquent'	92
'Larks are the sparks' (Song)	93

1950

'Oh shall I sing of Josephine?' (A Ballad)	94
'I'm as blind as a bat,' (Canon for three critics)	95
'Oh rose of sorrow'	96
'There was a man'	96

1951

'Thou, who grew so pure'	97
'Where's the poem?' (Solitude, 2)	98

1954

'There have been many; only one,' (Solitude, 3)	99

1955

'Lord Jesus once was' (Easter Lullaby)	100
'Whose blood is this' (A Canticle for Briony)	101

'Now the East Wind' 102
'No logical contradiction between us' 102

1956

'At twenty you were the distraction' (The Need) 103
'Why do you laugh up Your sleeve of night' (Solitude, 4) 104
'If I were a Prince' (Solitude, 5) 105
'To the lake of my aloneness' (Poem on a Painting, Solitude, 6) 105
'Murderers are merciful to me' (Solitude, 7) 106

1957

'Do me a favour, treat me with contempt;' (Solitude, 8) 109

1958

'Damn and blast you!' (Solitude, 9) 112
'I'm a psychic patient' (Instead of Mobile Worker) 113
'Autumn like a pheasant's tail' (Snapshot) 114
'Just as I used to wear your old sweater' (Solitude, 10) 115

1959

'He was a man of such considerable promise' (Epitaph for R.D., I) 116
'Searching for his anima' (Epitaph for R.D., II) 116
'Leaf that I am' (Solitude, 11) 117
'You have planted so many trees' (Solitude, 12) 117
'Lightly as willow leans over a river;' (Solitude, 13) 118
'Dearest, it is no longer true' (Solitude, 14) 118
'Her moss of sleep upon the bark of night' (Solitude, 15) 119
'Now that we love watch how the world conspires' (Solitude, 16) 119
'Dearest, since I cannot say why I love you' (Solitude, 17) 120
'As wet lilac bruised with scent' (Solitude, 18) 120
'In the forest of my dreams' (Epilogue) 121
'Why do you run away and kneel' (The Thought) 121
'You think this makes us equal: nothing will;' (Solitude, 19) 122
'Because I have looked into your eyes' (Solitude, 20) 122
'Loneliness is our thirst' (Solitude, 21) 122
'I have at last come to terms' (Solitude, 22) 123
'Does the wind move the branches' (Solitude, 23) 123

'Dearest, do me a favour' (Solitude, 24)	124
'Madam, if you are unaware' (Solitude, 25)	124

1960

'Most people are unhappy because they can't get what they need;' (Solitude, 26)	125
'It's all very disappointing: most disappointing.' (The Philanderer's Lament, Solitude, 27)	126
'What can I do with my love?' (Solitude, 28)	127
'Any man might miss' (Solitude, 29)	128
'All right, run off with you and go' (Solitude, 30)	129
'Dearest, be ruthless' (Solitude, 31)	130
'Words are a net' (Solitude, 32)	130
'Last night, my knees searched for you'	131
'Thou, on a Cross, I on a divided heart' (Solitude, 33)	131
'Because my eyes have stared' (Solitude, 34)	131
'I am as hungry as the Wind' (Wind Song)	132
'She, who's my music says'	132
'I spoke to my sadness and I said' (Solitude, 35)	133
'Easter'	133
'If you persist in concentrating'	133
'Today, I am sad,' (München-Gladbach Lyric)	134
'Lobes of mauve lilac' (Solitude, 36)	135
'Mountains are merciless as man' (Solitude, 37)	135
'As thrush, lark and linnet are' (Solitude, 38)	136

1961

'You ask me to write a poem' (Solitude, 39)	137
'There was no part of you' (Solitude, 40)	138
'Now that our love by life has been betrayed' (Solitude, 41)	138
'Since she whom I love' (The Gift)	139
'When all this place is rubble, ash and dross' (Postcard)	140
'She possesses me completely' (The Mistress)	140
'How fragile this frightened sparrow is' (Solitude, 42)	141
'If our ability to love' (Solitude, 43)	142
'How can we be parted' (Solitude, 44)	144

1962

'Here's the ground she and I, let our' (Clasp for a Mislaid Necklace)	146
'Where in this wide world can' (The Horse)	146

1964
'Excuse me, forgive me if I interrupt' (Poem written at the Request of a Political Group)   148
'You stand upon the lip of an abyss' (Lines for N.S.'s first birthday)   149
'How leaf we are' (Solitude, 45)   150

1965
'Where the earth floor was puddled with urine' (Carol)   151
'What falls more lightly' (Lullaby)   152
'At eighteen they are as Asia' (The Geography of Women)   153
'They tell you you're a pretty girl'   153
'I wish to ask you a question;' (To the Bishop of Coventry)   154
'Here where the modest water flows' (The Mill Leat)   155
'She lies propped up by pillows' (For a Dying Woman)   155
'If he were to walk into this cafe'   156
'Love is in the loving' (Solitude, 46)   157
'Handkerchiefs are the vultures' (Solitude, 47)   157
'In my time, I was here too,' (Solitude, 48)   158
'Our grief is not for his death'   158

1966
'Just as the same square-winged buzzard suddenly hunts'   160
'Sleep, my baby,' (Lullaby)   161

1967
'Whose boots are these' (The Survivors)   162
'I had hoped that' (Solitude, 49)   163
'My unhappiness had become a second skin to me:' (Solitude, 50)   163
'And he reached that point' (Solitude, 51)   164
'If you had died then death' (Solitude, 52)   164
'It rains behind my eyes' (Solitude, 53)   165
'Since nothing of itself can be' (Epithalmium)   165
'There have been many boats, many sailors before you' (For Sir Francis Chichester's return)   166

1968
'I am nothing, if not honest' (Solitude, 54)   168
'Our urchin love was brief;' (Solitude, 55)   168

'Come to me, Death,' (Solitude, 56)	168
'The tranquillity I find by this lake,' (The Lake)	169
'I ride, the road winds uphill' (Solitude, 57)	170
'Why is it when we ride together,' (Solitude, 58)	171
'Love passes; grief does not.' (Solitude, 59)	171
'Your death took everything from me but my life' (Solitude, 60)	172
'I would that my love should grow'	172

1969

'I have now become grateful for my worries,' (Solitude, 61)	173
'If gratitude is prayer' (Canticle)	174
'Truth is derived from events' (A Syllogism)	176
'Beside these bougainvilleas, Gandi fell' (In Delhi)	176
'When I peered into the bog of Irish history' (In Dublin)	177
'You ask me where we came from? I will tell you.' (Legend from Vancouver)	178
'Where quietness has roots; silence, leaves' (The Fraser Canyon)	179
'The purpose of life is to increase awareness, sensitivity,' (Envoi)	179
'Love like a storm breaks,' (Solitude, 62)	180
'If they should ask where he found beauty' (Solitude, 63)	180
'Confound your jealousy' (Solitude, 64)	181

1970

'A flock of flamingoes' (Spring Song)	182
'Here is a rose' (Lines for my daughter on her wedding day)	182
'Oblivion as a writer' (Solitude, 65)	183
'Rider, rein up your horse, let it graze' (Epitaph for Sir Mike Ansell)	183
'Who are all these grey little men'	184
'What a saboteur Time is' (Schubert)	185
'They tell me it's my birthday. How old am I?'	185
'If cities could speak' (Vancouver)	186
'For length: a ruler; for weight, a balance;' (Poetry)	187
'Last night I dreamt' (Solitude, 66)	188
'She, who in my heart' (Solitude, 67)	189
'Yet would that these words could give' (Solitude, 68)	189

'Damn and blast the middle classes' (Paprika, 1)	190
'Lenin, having forgotten his aims,' (Paprika, 2)	190
'I put my hand into my pocket' (Paprika, 3)	191
'St Thomas Aquinas wrote' (Paprika, 4)	191
'Mr Eliot informed me that he was convinced' (Paprika, 5)	192
'If there's a life after death' (Paprika, 6)	192
'Doctors are mere moles' (Paprika, 7)	193
'When I asked Dr Hill why he had become a psychiatrist' (Paprika, 8)	193
'Saints go to considerable lengths' (Paprika, 9)	194
'In England, honours come' (Paprika, 10)	194
'Be well advised' (Paprika, 11)	195
'Mr Harold Wilson says' (Paprika, 12)	196
'The U.S. Department of Justice considered' (Paprika, 13)	196
'Marriage is mutual cannibalism' (Paprika, 14)	197
'A Mr William Gaskill said' (Paprika, 15)	197
'When Pound was in clink' (Paprika, 16)	198
'Confound Tenessee Williams.' (Paprika, 17)	198

1971

'Neither health nor happiness' (Solitude, 69)	200

1972

'A jungle' (Solitude, 70)	201
'I know what it is I seek in you:' (Solitude, 71)	201
'You say you love me and imply' (Paprika, Ten Negatives, 1)	202
'You say you love me,' (Paprika, Ten Negatives, 2)	203
'When you say you love me,' (Paprika, Ten Negatives, 3)	203
'You say you love me' (Paprika, Ten Negatives, 4)	203
'You ask if I love you' (Paprika, Ten Negatives, 5)	203
'You ask me why I look so sad' (Paprika, Ten Negatives, 6)	203
'You give yourself to me' (Paprika, Ten Negatives, 7)	204
'Your vagina is like a sea anemone' (Paprika, Ten Negatives, 8)	204
'If only you had three breasts' (Paprika, Ten Negatives, 9)	204

'You claim you have given yourself to me' (Paprika, Ten
    Negatives, 10)   204
'What am I?' (Rogo Ergo Sum)   205

1973
'Must I, who've searched so long for her' (Solitude, 72)   206
'Though Earth lies heavy:'   206
'Now I mast high' (Solitude, 73)   207

1974
'She said: 'One of the advantages when you're about to
    die' (In Memoriam)   208
'As a baker, he went from house to house' (The Baker)   209
'Only because you ask me, will I write' (Solitude, 74)   209
'May this rose sheathed in Night'   210
'On wings of thought' (Omar Cayenne)   210
'Forgive my talent' (Forgive)   211
'Not for her beauty: that could be replaced' (The Reason)   212
'How eloquent her leaf gentle eyes are' (Solitude, 75)   212

1975
'What lamb's as gentle?' (Solitude, 76)   214
'As April perches' (Solitude, 77)   214
'Because a lady asks me' (Solitude, 78)   215
'Whose cruelty is this' (Solitude, 79)   217
'Remember me when I've no place,' (Solitude, 80)   218
'Wheels will wear acres in the ache of space' (Platform
    Postcard)   218
'Winter, slippered with leaves' (Winter)   219
'It is May: still days'   220
'Dear friends, be kind, abandon me' (The Envoi)   220
'He did not travel up the Amazon' (The Poet)   221
'Nothing unique can, or could exist;' (Post Script)   221
'I have come back again' (Solitude, 81)   222

1976
'The corn waits for its ripeness;' (Solitude, 82)   223
'What homes the swallow, makes'   223

xiv

'From where this crimson'	224
'Let me lie at the cliff edge outside this window;' (Instructions at my death)	225
'Thus weeps the rose and everything I see' (Inscription for a drawing)	225
'Autumn shawls the hill'	226
'Is life, this life, his life,' (Lament for Ben)	226
'Where the lyre to which these rows of vines' (Piesport)	227
'If they should ask you' (Solitude, 83)	227
'What seashell sleeves wave, surf or spray' (Solitude, 84)	228
'Does summer stride through the wide cornfields' (Summer)	229
'September shawls the shoulder of the year,'	230
'Keats trod here: no poet can follow' (Autumn)	230
'Oh bugger this. At this rate' (Requiem)	231
'Though I deny time reality,' (Solitude, 85)	232
'Just as an unmined ruby' (Solitude, 86)	233
'In the morning, I am sad;' (Solitude, 87)	233
'If pheasants head' (Canto, I)	234
'The West Ward holds six' (The Ward)	238
'Justice? What's justice? Did Jesus or Pilate' (Unrhymed Sonnets, 1)	240
'They say I am a shit because I commit' (Unrhymed Sonnets, 2)	241
'Acceleration is absolute; speed' (Unrhymed Sonnets, 3)	241
'Just as the Spring in tiny primroses speaks' (Unrhymed Sonnets, 4)	242
'Death be more proud. Don't stand outside her door' (Unrhymed Sonnets, 5)	242

1977

'My unkind heart, take pity on my heart' (Unrhymed Sonnets, 6)	243
'Marriage is nothing more than loneliness' (Unrhymed Sonnets, 7)	243
'What's a woman but a funnel' (Unrhymed Sonnets, 8)	244
'Who is there who has not sometime, somewhere' (Unrhymed Sonnets, 9)	244
'My unhappiness now crystallizes' (Unrhymed Sonnets, 10)	245

'Iago should have been a woman as' (Unrhymed Sonnets, 11)	246
'The ash and anguish of others' grief' (Unrhymed Sonnets, 12)	246
'Unless I can forgive I shall corrode' (Unrhymed Sonnets, 13)	247
'My health is going: my time almost gone' (Unrhymed Sonnets, 14)	247
'They talk of love as if it were a thing' (Unrhymed Sonnets, 15)	248
'I sit in an empty room, so crowded' (Unrhymed Sonnets, 16)	249
'By this bed in this vase' (Solitude, 88)	250
'Come to me promptly,' (Lines written by my mother's bed)	251
'No Easter egg, my child,'	252
'Sorry, no Easter egg'	252
'They say it is important to tell the truth' (Solitude, 89)	252
'Your leaving this morning' (Last Lyrics, 1)	253
'I sit alone' (Last Lyrics, 2)	253
'Ovid was driven from his home' (Last Lyrics, 3)	253
'If you could see my hand' (Last Lyrics, 4)	254
'Here's Milne: his feet cushions to his skull' (Epitaph for Milne)	255
'If I could rid myself of myself' (The Shell)	255
'It is early May' (Last Lyrics, 5)	256
'Both my fingers and the calendar' (Last Lyrics, 6)	256
'To-day an empty chair attacked me' (Last Lyrics, 7)	257
'Whether truth exists unless it is apprehended' (Truth)	257
'Do not believe the truth'	258
'Because of night' (Last Lyrics, 8)	260
'This rose weeps' (Last Lyrics, 9)	260
'They asked him' (Last Lyrics, 10)	261
'Wound of earth bandaged by night' (Last Lyrics, 11)	261
'With what precipitous grace' (Last Lyrics, 12)	261
'How snails the year' (Last Lyrics, 13)	262
'Autumn pheasants the hedge' (Last Lyrics, 14)	262
'Atlantic death waits' (Last Lyrics, 15)	263
'Winter ferrets knuckles of the banks,' (Last Lyrics, 16)	263
'Now silks the yellow on the daffodil,' (Last Lyrics, 17)	264

'Rampant lion haunches, fells the evening' (Last Lyrics, 18)	264
'The sky mooned with opals' (Last Lyrics, 19)	264
'By starred, violet tranquillity,' (Last Lyrics, 20)	265
'As a hand, the glove' (Last Lyrics, 21, The Parting)	265
'Dearest, in the autumn of my years' (Last Lyrics, 22)	265
'As a goldfish in a bowl' (Last Lyrics, 23)	266
'Now palms my hands above my sleepless eyes' (Last Lyrics, 24)	266
'The violet stars' (Last Lyrics, 25)	267
'He was a man with a handsome, wounded face'	267
'I stepped out into the dark. The timid deer of dawn' (Pastorale)	268
'Little girl, what is light?'	269
'With clouds as hands'	269
'Pheasants' feathers of amethyst,'	270
'Two telegraph posts: no wires between them'	270
'She bore a son'	271
'He kneels to his God,'	271
'Now wolf grief throats remorse,'	272
'To-day has been a sad day'	272
'The desert of your absence'	273
'If his love is all possessive'	273
'White wings scissor the linen air:' (Seascape)	273
'I am going where:' (Single Ticket)	274
'If this manoeuvring is love:' (Solitude, 90)	275
'Now sap squirts' (Spring)	275
'Galoshered, shuffling up the street'	276
'Taller than his shadow: a man' (Mike Ansell)	277
'Death said: 'Look at me' (The Anatomy of Death)	277
'For what jasmine of gentleness'	280
'Their curiosity lacks concern' (Women)	281
'With vines entwined upon the trellis of her sleep' (A Woman Sleeping on a Train)	281
'Elegant, immaculately turned-out' (A Woman of Fashion)	282
'You ask the question' (For a Growing Girl)	283

1978

'Why do I flee from you, since you pursue' (A Friend)	284
'Greedy Earth, who now devours my own Mother'	285

'Black earth whites her bones'	285
'Who is this friend I can ignore' (The Dog)	286
'If sleep is the way' (Ethel Duncan)	287
'Here lies my Mother' (Epitaph)	287
'The Felucca is a slender-necked bird' (The Felucca)	288
'Egypt a nation with only its past before it' (Egypt)	288
'The Thebans have conquered'	289
'The trouble from being as intelligent as I am' (The Quandary)	290
'They are all either' (Barnstaple)	290
'Dearest, I have an admission to make,' (Solitude, 91)	291
'Though I do not know you personally'	292
'Do not believe I loved you' (Solitude, 92)	293
'I am dying' (Rondo 'La Clemenza di Tito')	293
'A lost demented nomad, he misspent his life' (Solitude, 93)	294
'Child, who birthed in gentle June'	295
'Here Igor and Ez lie beneath their eiderdown of stone:' (In Memoriam)	295
'Per Piazzale Roma: Alla Ferrovia: Per Piazza San Marco:' (Death in Venice)	296
'Butterfly dreams unfurl'	296
'If those rodents who've gnawed or ignored my work'	297
'How leaf we are; these autumn years'	297
'Stables: a National Trust Shop:' (Cotehele)	298
'Music's no food, Olivia, it's a poison' (Solitude, 94)	299
'Dearest, promise to be merciful to me now' (Solitude, 95)	299
'The city darks, shadowed, lamp lit' (Plymouth)	300
'An old man widdling down his leg' (Winter's song)	301
'Grief is not something we give the dead' (Dirge)	301
'Now my glad eyes butterfly and rise,' (On Summer)	302
'But when we forgive' (Solitude, 96, Agnus Dei)	303
'Dearest, be kind deprive me utterly,' (Solitude, 97)	303
'You want to know what love is?' (Solitude, 98)	304
'Dearest, your absence' (Solitude, 99)	304
'Where have her opal eyes flown?' (Solitude, 100)	305
'The reason I have not written' (Solitude, 101)	306
'My mind mothed by jealousy' (Solitude, 102)	306
'The result of having'	307
'What is this rose?' (The Rose)	308

'The notion held by scientists, philosophers and theologians'	308
'Who was it who nudged me when I sat lonely' (Epitaph for a Friend)	309
'What love is this I feel for you?' (Franz Schubert)	309
'Only the deaf dare listen to Schubert'	311
'A navvy with hobnail boots'	311
'Sleep blackbirds and bears'	312

1979

'What is sex?'	313
'I do not wish to caress the coral of your breasts:' (Solitude, 103)	314
'This is spiritual vandalism'	314
'What is love?' (A Happy Poem)	315
'What is shame?'	316
'Your cruelty was you were so kind' (Solitude, 104)	316
'Come back to me' (Solitude, 105)	316
'Forget my anger' (Solitude, 106)	317
'Help me, dear God, to die'	317
'There is a necessity for prayer,' (Canto, II)	318
'Arms across eyes, I stand; face against wall.' ('Who is the I?')	319
'Gamow's Big Bang and Bondi's Steady State theories' (Canto, III)	320
'Love is not a gift, but an achievement' (Canto, IV)	323
'When we are young old age is a period' (Canto, V)	324
'What is it but hope' (Hope Canto, VI)	325
'Faith, a fugitive, hounded by reason' (Faith Canto, VII)	326
'Why don't you ever write anything happy?' She once asked' (Happiness Canto, VIII)	327
'Grief is not death's demesne' (Grief Canto, IX)	329
'Jealousy is the proof of love, they tell me' (Jealousy Canto, X)	331
'I, who had backed the black,' (Forgiveness Canto, XI)	333
'It is an occupied country' (Canto, XII)	334
'He who has not been tempted to take his own life' (Canto, XIII)	335
'If time is motion' (Solitude, 107)	336
'Since the present is invisible'	337
'Ambition, an horizon' (Ambition Canto, XIV)	338

'You from the depths; I, from the shallows' (From the shallows, Canto, XV) 339
'Value me no less' (Solitude, 108) 342
'It is when we feel that we have been betrayed' (Solitude, 109) 342
'Nature is no consolation:' 343

Date unknown

'With silent wings' (Solitude, 110) 344
'Oh when will the encircling bird of sleep' (Lullaby) 344
'In the centre of his brain' (Nocturne) 345
'From where these birds' (The Magnolia) 345

INDEX 347

Introduction

Ronald Duncan was born in 1914. His concern for the plight of England in the thirties led him to the Peace Pledge Union, and collaboration with Benjamin Britten rather than the left wing bandwagon. At the age of twenty-two, when he had completed the English Tripos under Dr F. R. Leavis at Cambridge, he visited Gandhi in India and lived with him on his Ashram for several months. Gandhi has undoubtedly been a principal influence on Duncan.
After his return to England in 1937 he settled on the North Devon Coast near Bideford where he still lives. Towards the end of the war he resumed his collaboration with Britten to produce the libretto for THE RAPE OF LUCRETIA (first produce at Glyndebourne in 1946). At the same time his conviction that, as poetry is language at its most intense, it is therefore the most effective medium for the drama led him to compose the verse play THIS WAY TO THE TOMB (1946). STRATTON (1948), DON JUAN (1953), THE DEATH OF SATAN (1954) and THE CATALYST (1956) followed.

What is the purpose of poetry? I can find no better answer than Ronald Duncan's:

> 'For human consciousness; poetry;
>   it is the instrument of definition,
> The marking out of distinctions, the extension of territory
>   which the mind can cultivate and colonize.
> The words: a swipe at the jungle,
>   the inarticulate undergrowth;
> the right words: a sharp sickle
>   precisely fashioned'

Duncan admits that he is a disciple of Donne regarding form and clarity. He is convinced that a poem written in a 'tight' verse form increases its impetus rather than impedes it. He apologizes that he writes poetry 'because I'm lazỳ and I'd rather send a telegram than write a letter', but the lines:

> 'Remember me,
>   And do not grieve,
> When I am ash
>   for the wind to weave.'

have very much more impact than a ten page letter.

Duncan's concern with the development of human consciousness has stimulated him to write MAN (which is not included in the collection). In this epic poem he has made a bridge across the abyss between the arts and sciences and composed Cantos on such subjects as: the origin of life, the development of language, the history of the earth and the geometry of space. He remarks that 'Eliot and Pound have freed poetry of poetic language; I am trying to free it of poetic subjects'.

The poems in this collection span fifty-one years. Duncan wrote his first poem when he was fourteen. Although he has written his autobiography he regards these poems (together with MAN) as his most serious work.

Miranda Weston-Smith

Editorial Note

I have attempted, with the help of the author, to arrange the poems in this collection in chronological order. At the beginning of each section for a particular year I have placed those poems for which an exact date is known. The last part of this book contains poems whose date of composition I have been unable to trace. I have numbered the Solitudes in chronological order and so this system will differ from those previously used.

I feel the chronological order of the poems imposes the minimum editorial interference. Naturally the poems reflect alterations in mood, style and tempo over the years. I have wished to leave the interpretation of these to each reader.

1928

Danse Macabre

Huge cliffs shoulder the sea. You can
keep your – paintings and poetry!
And music......?
Listen, you can't lose it.

Someday soon, I shall get tired
Of this coming back with its persistent buttoning.
I shall get tired, loose-jawed asking them to play,
   my way.

As the days repeat,
As the weeks complete,
As months filed and forgotten retreat
from my mind's meaning,
So my untidy day-dreamings hurl me along,
harden till I hold
dust, as you wake me, pull me together,
teach what I know.

Already the waves reach
well in my sleep
I will lie down near the waves.
Soon, I shall be gone from here.

Shall I tell, or let the sea say?
Must I struggle and sweat, so you can
forget the words I wrote out
to tell you my way?
Or shall I let the sea say,
let the sea say?

Well watch the weed in the water
lilt, nearly
lie down, as each wave washes
well over it, tearing its leather leaves,
teasing: – Well, what can I have to say?

1928

1929

Canzone: The River

It is of woman's love I sing
Which flows to man like a great river;
To deserts of desire it brings
The graceful ease of a full river
Which slakes my thirst with its clean wine
And yielding gives till all is mine,
    And she, with my own thirst, combines.

As blue height to a lark gives wing,
Or as spring rain falling fills a river,
So does her love grow by giving
Till I am drowned within that river,
Yet breathe an air there crystalline
Through her wet lips incarnadine
    Which drink my thirst till I recline

As a tired leaf which falling
Falls to float upon a flooded river
Or as a white swan gliding
Through the night – but is not night a river,
And our days, deserts where we pine,
For woman's love which flows like wine
And generous as a river?

                                              1929

1931

Tempusque Virgo

Life's easy for her:
People pay her taxis,
Asked to lunch, dinner, and tea,
yet retains her virginity.
Taking from many, she gives to none,
Mingy with love, she finds life fun. – Unfortunately,
one of her suitors, a well-known fellow,
has plenty to spend, and patience to wait
in any weather.
Well, this one, will have her – gradually.

1931

1933

Had We The Time

When men hunger and women
willow,
they place their thumbs on immortality;
forge perpetual bodily desire.
Our true significance seems to lie
in propagation.
Let's analyse our souls, or what it is,
   (that we neglect on earth
   to live with ever after)
Are they much more than the pip of desire,
the impatient throb through us?
We could create such loveliness –
   strengthen our immortality –
     if we had time,
       had we the time.

                                1933

For Continuity

I can remember my Mother's womb,
The slow surge of strength, of consciousness
the sudden change of feeling turned, withdrew into touch
touch of flesh other than my own,
the hours of forced wakefulness, of uneasiness;
    the beginning to be,
    the beginning of my captivity.
Then, as your blood pushed through me, quickened me,
    my limbs awoke,
    our contact broke:
frightened, that I should lose you,
I thrust myself from you
hoping thus to find you.
    Swaddled in pain,
    clutching in vain:
    formed from your heart,
    to be, to strive apart.

1933

Who really loves me?
No-one.
Relatives, you know me,
Friends, you owe me.
Who really loves me?
No-one.

1933

Confessio Amantis

It was as if I'd met the Lord,
confessed to him,
stood while he stared;
then, saw him laugh,
and merely walk away.

1933

1934

Aria

Because I enjoy a solitary tree
more than a forest –
a cedar of Lebanon
   stark on a hill at a slant
means to me much more
than any cluttered copse or well-spaced wood.
I do appreciate the family man's position;
though he loses the intermittent
windthrill,
he makes up for it, certainly,
    in immediate access to
    in recess, safe.
           Blanket security.
Shall we dance?

1934

1935

I

The earth's excited with leaf and labour,
See! It calls on this river to flow more fully,
   bulge out lock gates, circulate
the heavy fields, lifting with quickened spring.

II

You've measured my rise, but forgotten my flow.
You no longer loiter along me,
Stand, stare, feel, know what I've given you.
   Yearly I've given you.
You no longer loiter along me.

III

Between two banks; hope and despair
You decide and flow.
You build bridges and burrow me,
facilitate a one way stream of traffic.
Success or forgetfulness –
You no longer loiter along me

IV

Thousands of hands
Clutch into the morning,
Airing the city's sheets,
Thousands of hands crawl
As sand crabs crawl,

rubbed red hands crawl across
table cloths, laying methodically and setting alarms.
Clocked in postponement of serial dreams,
Pumice reality.
Your life punctuated by time signals,
Everything measured but left unnoticed,
Shadows locked up in the glare,
Half-light vanished by embankment lighting.
You make gloves
With gloves on.

V

Is there none left there, then?
None.
No, listen, though life leans from us,
there's strength in us to stretch back,
and fasten feelers where we want to wait.
None? Then, loiter along me.
Look at the flow, and then follow.
Water in dreams tell,
(if we tell our dreams)
birth, the beginning, Deirdre – dead?
No! touch here in the almond tree.
Feel?
Or the horses' hot shoulder, and sudden eyes, see!
Undress life, plunge
my depths of infinite buoyancy.

VI

When a duck hangs dead,
its blood runs red,
fills up the beak, full
overflows, falls out red.
Ducks on the stream float
beaks hidden in wing,
warm feathered throat,
fluffed in the wind, water lapped, strong.

1935

Insignificance

I turned in time to see a star, stretch
On infinity, and far
Across the taut and vapid sky
It chalked its way,
Slitting the darkness with an edge of light
Dissolving instantly, weighed down with night;
Then slowly, like blood oozing, shapes and noises
Seemed to hold their hands together, nudge their presence into sight.
Just as before the waves
Repeated phrases, told them backwards, scissoring around hysteria,
Still consoling, soothing and patting indecision:
They could not tell, or didn't see
A star scratch heaven, show my significance to me.

1935

Mr Holy Ghost

When may I introduce to you
the child in me weeping
to know you?
He, whose gloves my hands are,
   whose shoes my feet are,
   whose eyes my eyes are.
He, we, out of the one window stare
   my grin imprisoning him

Oh Mary! You are his Mother,
  he, for his Mother,
    will have
    no other
I, Mary, will have no other
If you Mary will be Mother.

                              1935

Parish Church

'The Blessed Sacrament said here
Is for the sick, the needy –
  and the poor people of this parish.
Will those who enter first kneel and pray,
then, as they pass out, not forget
to give,
  to give a penny to the poor of the parish . . .
nor forget those amongst us – who are infirm . . .'

But we haven't time,
and there's not much room,
by the gaudy altar
and the spacious tomb;
to make up a prayer
to cross off the poor,
the patient queue at the Chancel door . . .

Let a prayer be said
for the comfortable dead;
But for those kept poor,
what prayers can be said?
– Apologetically said in a tight-lipped mutter
as we knee a fat hassock near this gilded clutter.
Beneath these windows that keep out the light
(By Sir Arthur given' . . . to put him right)

Windows that only show the picture inside
(A Good Wise Man on a donkey ride)
... 'For the poor of this parish
    let us pray'...

No! let us sing!
    let us swear!
        let us swing through the air.
There's no prayer for the poor
      that can feed
        to their need.
    Prayers for the dead
    Bread for the paupers!

Let us sing!
    Let us swear!
        Out! Out! to the generous Virgin – to the air!

                              1935

1936

Question

Do what Rimbaud
                 did – eh?
Chuck it!
And leave the old women who clutter round Leavis,
With a horse and a tree, music my idolatry,
   drug myself with the meaning of meaning.
Or take up a cause
   to delay wars?
Join a society
To banish propriety?
Look underdone
To make women pity?
Take up a gun, drink beer in the city?
Or shall I decide to fight?
   Yes, I'll write!
   I'll write till they read it.
   They'll need it!
   They'll need it!
   Believe it! Believe it!
   I'll write till they read it!

                             7 May 1936

Poem

Not in the swing of the year
nor in the swish of the season's skirt
vaulting the earth's spray disclosing
   mobile blues innumerable, innumerable.
Not in this thing, nor in that thing
in between or around the fingers and toes of spring
in summer's broad brimmed abandon
or in autumn's loaded lap, had he found Him
So he cut god's name in an apple
and planting the pips in the sky
flung the rind over his shoulder
cursing the worn word god and all god's paid preachers
vowing he'd hunt with the wind and follow the women
rather than runt like a pig in a sty
poking for meat out of theology's paving.
Wind took him and women took him
while the pip grew to a tree to an orchard
there his tired bones sit under his life's branches,
with his god, where he cannot die.

                                                      1936

After Dinner Speech

It is essential that an ultimatum should be sent
To Utopia. We must inform her Government,
Immediately, that we can no longer stand
These sacrifices, which we continually make

To our unemployed.
   May the exiled citizens of Utopia remember
This: – Britain can, if necessary, defend herself
From herself. There is every possibility of a
Revival in trade (failing which
Some European War could be arranged
To alleviate the monotony for our less-fortunate
Leisured brothers)
But, let me say: Patience in Poverty makes for Prosperity.
The unemployed is certainly a serious problem,
But there are others, – We must face them.

                                                                    1936

Epigram

   Knowing that a cock or a bull
   can suggest more modestly than words can do,
   he took the woman out to the country;
   shewed her
      the brown earth's green increase,
   and she wisely,
      promised to give her love
      as she took her breath –
   naturally;
   but then spotting the green earth's loose decline
   she decided to preserve herself
      for death – a rival, not in his original design.

                                                                    1936

The Panther

Night like a lean leopard
sprang through the trees
sat on my lap
elephant.
Heaviness of smoothness,
fatness of blackness,
beat in breast of love or
udder of life or
skirt swing of Mother?
Which, I cannot tell; but it quietens me.
Till I weaned, weary of peace, pace
turn face
lick lap and painful eye
crouched panther drinking my shadow down.
His sides swell with each swallow.
Till the insidious dog day
yapped and my panther slunk away.

1936

Passion's No Prince

Passion's no prince,
   is the maimed mind's blindness;
bog, where the brain
   struggles to womb slunkfulness, nothingness,
and dreams revenge in dreams.
Veins cross, intricate chaos.
Blood's insect busyness
   catacombs the mind's enamelled vacancy.

And to this hall, the heart
   with rigid ceremony
comes beating its welcome
on its own ridiculous drum.
There, in the grave,
the heart lets down its full skirt of bones,
and in enveloping nakedness,
unpillars the brain's hall,
breaks each phallus of thought,
enjoys a tight privacy,
is sick; satisfied;
            is passionate; dead.

                                          1936

1937

Poet 1937

The maddening traffic of my dreams
   takes toll, tears
at the lid of sleep, wears
deep tar-marks, grit scratch or skid
   swerve across ticket-strewn 'oatmeal rooms'
till my nerves
         vibrate hate
         and I wake
worn to a torn up
poster-plastered day tasting of petrol fumes
and clever selling motor-bike-ideas
dead.
   Tom-tom reiteration
   sells the best interpretation.
Then fear's slick gears
         change and grate –
giving only brief
pneumatic-lorry-relief.
         As a dream's deceit's neat
so the day's delirium
         leaves no lane
for hysterical herds of sensitive words
   to loiter along, form in a file...
But from such snap-shot pastoral scenes,
You must interpret my heart's tense,
And make meaning of
         my mind's metaphor.

Jou-Jou
(for E. E. Cummings)

Were the curls
curves of skin
protruding through muslin,
line of thigh,
circle her eye-
balls (reflecting me)
circumferotion, waveface,
motion, fingers,
Donne and the 22 Sonata.....
   'Thy centre is' – which reminded me,
So after argument, worn the heard words were,
   slippersaying,
     I said: 'I like your bum better than Mexico
        Your breasts as oranges or alps are
        The rest as Seattle is,
        But I must to St. Cloud.'

                                      1937

Spring is no certain thing:
   spite of the bulb's dry tightness till
   metamorphosis to
   tulip's wet-lip looseness,
Spring is no certain thing.
   The perennial push through the almond's laughter of lather
   draws only snapshot applause;
   Show of hands from unanimous daffodils
   merely moves us to plate glass fashions, cinema passions;
Spring is no certain thing.

                                      1937

Across the desert
innumerable echoes of desires, fears –
beat ceaseless reverberation on automatic drums.
Above the swamps
sweat of argument.
Uncolonised continents beneath the sea,
hear dry whispers of mortality.

We have wired up our wilderness
but the wind through the wires
only makes our wilderness wider, wilder ...
– It is extraordinary – what science can do.

1937

Let's speak around and about yesterday,
   or of tomorrow talk of:
for I move we ignore today for:
   the creaking stalks of this confident spring,
are enough to enliven or annoy any man's bones,
   or lever his set skeleton;
let alone, leave his grazing brain alone from
   suck-worrying.
A single bluebell's certain thrust
   through the clogged up leaf dust,
Or even lift of a linnet will allow for
   distraction from, action for, moral satisfaction;
The pops of spring haven't got anything to do with
   push of progress;
Squeeze inside almond or larch
   less to do with struggle for
                    ordered expansion to spacious vacuity
than a cow's tail on tea pot.
   Guess, the by-pass worlds of tomorrow
must be planned for by dead men
   while the live are lost to the living.

1937

Song Of The Earth

Oh earth, I am in love with thee:
as with a woman, I am in love with thee.
I press my face to your cliff-flanks and cry
oceans, wide oceans of tears till skin chaffs dry.
My abundant blood forces
   your rivers courses.
My bone your mountains marrow, mine.
Your joy my fountain's fur.
    Limp my sorrow fill
   your valley, your hill.
Oh earth, I am in love with thee
as with a woman, I am in love with thee.

1937

1938

Our Difficulty Is

Give me your hand.
I see you: know;
then let our lips
know.
   Say something; your silence
frightens: why do you lie, still?
   Say something, say something.
Is all: said?
He hasn't: said.
Hold hard his head:
hard his head.
Only he at home now
only he at ease: pleased.
Making his pleasure pain,
                    again pain
burrowing back to anchor me
trap me
keep me where
I was torn from born.
Our difficulty is
            with your eyes:
                        only,
So let me,
      I must rise,
                forget me.

                                    1938

I Worry How To Tell My Love

I worry how to tell my love
Since she
   my love allowed.
When there was doubt about it,
how it would shout about it, till she
   to quieten me,
   regave me, me
   out of her womb's vacuity.
Now in a summer of certain sun
steep flowers of, fall back, bent
   with no comment, – satiety's loquaciousness.
Translate the inarticulate?
Continent defying measurement.
My eyes' empire cedes from my lips alliance
the words, worn;
   phrases pulped into cinema headlines ...
I worry how to tell my love
Since she my love allowed.

                                                            1938

Plain Song

   The revolving Earth
   tunes into one of the four seasons
   to tease our incompatible desires.
      Spring amplifies our hunger;
      Summer tones down our appetite:
      Autumn records our disappointment;
      and Winter sets us in silence again.

Oh, Earth, busy with fertility,
   wheat and the woman,
   turn and attend to;
   those who are uprooted,
   whose blood wastes into
   warm bathwater apathy –
who with sad frivolity ignore each season,
pursuing comfort for an uncomfortable reason.

                                          1938

I Wonder If Her Wise, Wide Eyes

I wonder if her wise, wide eyes
   merely threw out, shew,
      what her blood thinks about, knows?
Or whether the look, the stare there tries
from sheer fear to hide, ignore
store of, race river of grace, piped up inside
still? Well, several of the sides, the point's permanent.
And there's no ruse, excuse, trick, nick in her look –
only easy, leaf liberal,
compliment to lip,
as woods weeds have,
wind speed,
and my love
       its need, greed, need.

                                          1938

Song

Sooner or later, you
or some other
body, will love me
or let me love.
We in long grass pursue
whole hours of abandon through:
leisurely, let our lust recline,
        let our love decline
till I in you, and you are mine.

                              1938

Song

The clean shy leaves undress the trees
wondering: whether the weather
effort of grace laced to embarrassment,
is worth the
dirt, neglect, disappointment,

And there are a few girls, one or two,
who
      could enjoy joy
         give live
whose blood's beauty is gloved,
shoved dirty – disease –
ease of convenience
so why sing?

So the boy, Ronnie,
escaped for a day,
found the sure gorse,
fingered it,
bled, fled,
forced a few words down
   an avenue of unheeding cedars
—shortly to be sold for, to make way for:
our growing population.

                                        1938

1939

Unfinished Eulogy

Her birthday, – up she gets, she's twenty three;
   Oh well, that's what she tells me;
Either she lies, or history cheats
Or were Troy's beauties also Time's deceits,
   And Helen's counterfeit?
For if beauty does not die, nor can she
Therefore her age must be eternity, –
   which doesn't surprise me.
For Dante knew her and Villon loved her
(inside of Paris) and didn't Chaucer
   See her and wink at her?
Donne's mistress proving her inconstancy;
She sneaks from Marlow's bed to bounce with me,
   (Rousing Pound's jealousy).
The point and balance of her strict features
requires an exact focus; a picture
   – insulates the creature.
Blast it! my pen sticks its heels in and won't budge
at the word 'beauty'; word my ears might nudge
   out for my hand to smudge
Out with all the slack terminology
Of Mr Eliot's theology,
   and Murray's apology
For Christ, and Leavis' crush on Lawrence.

Gawd! what a bum age do I sit in, since
   dumbness has lost its silence.
When I could be getting the Star's harvest
in ... at least half my time spilt! And the best
   sheaves rattled down: lost
Because the rims of the verbs are rotten,
Adjectives rusty, and the shafts broken ...
   verse at a stiff price again?
Well, let's start at the top of her, with her hair,
It's plentiful and what's more it's fair, –
   (Well, what's at the top of her).
Her eyes: blue, – that's no matter, but they will
Leap, thread and follow you, are never still;
   Leopards crouch on their window-sill.
And where her lips are a turquoise serpant sits
shedding a scarlet skin, then letting its
   suppleness to our kiss, fit.

                                       1939

Phallic Song

I

'For an old reason
I ring new words, because
   She in a fresh face
   finds Love's old form,
      accepts me,
      rejects me,
      comes and withdraws,
      according to Love's rigid laws, –
which I would keep
   if I could keep
this ruler, prisoner with me.'

                                       1939

Looney's Song

The girl at the factory took me in,
So I took the girl from the factory out.
The girl from the factory let me in
When I'd forgotten –
                what I'd called about.

1939

1940

Postcard

Today the Vicar came down – it being Good Friday, –
asked to church.
Sit in his dressed up mausoleum
and listen to his dull chatter?
A fidgety little man
itching to do
something he daren't do
and I can't do for him.
So I got the old flour barrel out
and creosoted it
the sun made it shine: belly of a basuto;
and, thanks to Messrs Chivers, I unearthed a jar.
I pulled out a chair full of daffodils.
For God?
Well, it rinsed my eye.

                                              1940

Night creeps
like a sleek cat
soft, swift, silent:
pads, paws, laps, licks
light spilled from evenings shallow saucer,
slowly withdraws satisfied, fed –
and the full darkness purrs up, out at me.

1940

Phallic Song
II

Strong as the Nelson Column and with no pigeons on it;
tireless
as tubes on the Bakerloo,
– and keeps to a safe schedule;
gentle
as weak things aren't
sure as the elephant;
Where the hell's the garage
for this Golden car?
Lidy, d'you
know of a convenient parking place?

1940

Experiment With Old Metaphors

Veins can, as vines climb, swell,
will fill, whether you allow
                            or let
    push of growth be
                         grip of pain.
Veins can't, as eyes can, forget:
Veins must, as eyes won't, veins fret.
    In vain, fat grapes of grief fall.
Vine, my love, learns
                        nothing at all,
    for it is set so,
    must grow so, though
you allow
          or let
trunk of my tree, me, reaching bones, all,
fall, to be, become, sum: bleaching skeleton sunk
by side you, woman, wall
free
but for the shadow of these lines on thee.

                                              1940

Song To Sea

    Isn't there something in common
        between us?
    You, with your restless reaching
        incessant striving;
    – superficial show of strength –
    and inside listlessness?

                                                1940

Hayharvest Song

Sheaves of grass,
gathered at last;
In spite of the rain,
We have sheaves again.

1940

1941

Feast Of Sowing

Let us start here: for this, is where we are.
If we begin here, it will save moving and lifting
   eyes walking up hill and hearts walking down hill.
Let us start here
   whilst we are by a miracle for a moment together.

We have returned here after worshipping
innumerable and invisible gods,
We have prayed for these in words
words whilst weeds grew in our garden.
And now we have come back,
clumsy as bullocks;
and we stand here thinking:
This is an awkward affair
                    when will the feast start
and someone is mumbling:
      'it is wrong to deify the soil
        that gods' feet are not clay feet
     and that this is an attempt to construct a ritual,
                            amateur Theology.'
Oh Ceres, sister, say:
Have I not stood here for a thousand years?
The soil waits: here's seed for it:
   oats, peas and beans, five bushels to the acre, some for the crow
Let the feast start. We'll harrow to-morrow.

                                        May 1941

1942

Canzone

I

Love like a dog barks
              at the heel of my leisure,
yaps, teases my schemes,
    and all my dreams,
        brings all straight,
wherever they graze or wait,
      even my blood runs to her
And her live eyes mark
      the quick strength and measure
of this heart which seems
    to beat extremes,
        loves then hates,
is never moderate,
      changeable as the weather.

And what her wet lips say softly, her eyes ignore,
and therefore
   there is division in her state
making a quick debate,
   and she does nothing,
and so allows him to serve her there, and bring

To her luminous womb an impatient emperor
who is more
than anxious to inherit his estate
before he abdicates;
    while I on her smooth skin
press grateful lips, then bite my suffering.

II

And behind her head
stands our patient ancestry:
ghosts, all our forbears,
they wait and stare
    inactive,
whilst we in furious joy, live,
and allow them their release,
through our veins and bed;
    for the child we make gaily,
runs to a tomb where
    eyes, mouth and hair,
        the dead give
their representative
        for a period, a lease

Of searching, like haphazard travellers
who never
know their way and are all fugitives
from their objective,
which is the womb and the grave, where
we at last reach our first and second mother.

And here she lies like a graceful river,
and now her
    hand moves and is restive,
a restorative,
    and her thighs' sepulchre
yield new relics for her breasts' cool cloister.

III

Now a hospital
with lawns and flowers and bees,
and the loud silence
of slow suspense,
    and anxious
visitors timidly curious,
and laughter from the kitchen
falls like a cymbal
of a server's sneeze;
then time's indifference
is most intense,
minutes are ponderous,
and this and that's an omen,

Till a bell perforates the corridor,
and a door
opens and is shut on us,
and brisk nurses without fuss
    bring bowls of water;
she tugs at a towel: she groans like a heifer;

Till it lies wet, on her thigh
she sweats from labour;
and they pour water
and smear its rigorous

limbs with numerous
ointments; it murmurs,
and missing the warm womb, cries in a temper.

IV

Whose birth is this and
whose death is this, is this
birth my death and she,
the child, is she,
    my shadow
and I her son's embryo?
    Whose immortality
whose eyes and whose hand
whose metamorphosis?
My father's? Is he,
    through her, set free
from photos
and from death's packed depot,
set to dance in her *jeu d'esprit*,

From his unmarked standard grave on which a cactus grew
and a few
weeds waved pink flowers in the dry sirocco?
– her fingers are just so –
and it's strange to look where
the child's eyes are and see one's grandmother.

This birth and any death makes an impromptu interview
with God, apropos
oneself; *quid pro quo*
our terms, and His
where our minds are not but our hearts loiter.

V

In blind worm wisdom;
    in river affluence
threshed grain generous,
    voluptuous;
        as wheat falls,
sprawls on the floor liberal,
    or as seed to the soil's lust
falls, is not lost, comes
    back to its essence
to its first focus,
    and is vigorous,
        prodigal:
wheat, man and woman, all
    must submit so, which is just.

This I did. For there is no alternative
but passive
sacrifice: to be the feast at the festival,
the corpse at the funeral;
    else one sits chewing an idea,
an unconverted infidel to one's own dull dogma.

And so we love, in order that we may live,
and we give
our life away. Now, I dare not close my eyes
for fear of seeing you
    nor open them to know you are not there.

Envoi

Now you can go, Canzone, in your new suit
which I have made to your own strict measurement
and precise arrangement
making my impatient heart fit
to your fixed limit;
Those who dress to please the fashion
may turn their arse to you: kick it with passion!

1942

Poems From The War

I

Noticing that one of our randy guns
was enjoying itself with the nave of Narvik cathedral,
and had, at that precise moment, ejected considerable shrapnel
through the side of Our Lord Jesus Christ;
and as an encore
perforated the Virgin's pinafore,
I suggested to our Captain in charge
that this sort of activity
was unlikely to preserve a nation's liberty ...
He replied, with some wit,
'Does cricket?'

1942

Poems From The War

II

Ah well! all these sailors
sinking to heaven
with more ease than a porpoise could
cause widowhood.

A spruce gull
lands on the unsubmerged belly of the late Herr Rauschmidt
and pecking a button off, leaves Baruch's compliments of
the season i.e. shit.

1942

The Miller's Lament
(After Dunbar)

I who had sound health and a wife
sharing the dust and sweat of life
am now lonely, sick and full of misery.
    Timor mortis conturbat me.

She who was my joy and gladness
is now taken from me by great sickness
and lies in all weathers, decays patiently.
    Timor mortis conturbat me.

It is not wise to love too well.
I did this and watched my own funeral
and walked home to a dog's dumb pity.
    Timor mortis conturbat me.

If I had had no wife, lived alone
cooked my own grub, or stayed at home
I would have missed this master tragedy.
    Timor mortis conturbat me.

We love from weakness, I can see;
Love's an indulgence – You and me
pay for our pleasure – death's high usury.
    Timor mortis conturbat me.

Now like my donkeys in harness
I plod up and down in sadness
Haltered and hobbled by her memory.
    Timor mortis conturbat me.

For each thing she did, I must do;
where she put this, there must I too
or else offend, which is not kind of me.
    Timor mortis conturbat me.

Fools think they are free; an old man
knows better than this, for he can
see his own tail as his own tyranny.
    Timor mortis conturbat me.

Our efforts here melt like a wad of snow.
We come in poor and poor we go.
Of what use my midnight industry?
    Timor mortis conturbat me.

To own my own farm at thirty
That was my aim, and now seventy
even my bum is the bank's security.
    Timor mortis conturbat me.

So I leased the Mill, and carried
sack after sack, and worried
water to work more, clouds rain more for me.
    Timor mortis conturbat me.

I, fool, worked all day, and at night
sent my poor wife on shift till light:
which explains why I have no family!
    Timor mortis conturbat me.

Bearings well greased, stones sharp set,
the belts resined, the floor just wet
catches a bit of my neighbour's barley.
    Timor mortis conturbat me.

    And I cajoled a cat
    who habitually sat
    with a lecherous smile
    on my side on the scale!
    The trick worked wonders
    for the cat weighed well –
    – well bushels and bushels of barley meal
    it must have took
    to keep her up
    with her lecherous smile
    on my side of the scale.
      Till the farmers of Bradworthy
      full of ale and fury,
      those pagan fellows
      without Christian scruple,
      limping with laughter and lusting for slaughter
    used my own Mill wheel for my own cat's gallows.
      Timor mortis conturbat me-ow!

All this great effort of cunning
this lifting and greasing and cheating
went to buy a parcel of land close by.
    Timor mortis conturbat me.

The meal from the floor fed the pigs;
and I carried dung from the hogs
to nurse up this land – a brave step from the sty!
    Timor mortis conturbat me.

I coaxed this sour marsh, I drained it,
I dunged it, I ditched it, I limed it;

Pigs best, graves next, improve fertility.
   Timor mortis conturbat me.

It was all coming back to a pasture
a fair good pick for a heifer
and now rabbits spawn over my husbandry.
   Timor mortis conturbat me.

There I planned to build a cow house
there I would build my farm house
if I had time, which I had not, a pity.
   Timor mortis conturbat me.

Yet each tide that flowed, I followed
for beams, lintels – tons I collared
whereas four good boards would have done for me.
   Timor mortis conturbat me.

Ambition's half blind, sees things done
before they're thought of, or begun
with hands stiff tired and over-worked donkeys.
   Timor mortis conturbat me.

My unfinished farm, all its schemes
and half-made gates, collapse and seem
to move to my grave's simplicity.
   Timor mortis conturbat me.

My Mill wheel broken; buckets bust;
Rats in riotous living inherit all;
and assiduous spiders turn prodigal.
An antique now. And rust and dust
devour screens, belts, scales and even me. –
All slide into a picturesque eternity.
   Timor mortis conturbat me.

Damn Spillers' oily affluence!
Confound inventions of indolence
and Combine Millers! Oh bugger Electricity!
For barn threshers and oil – these ruined me.
   Timor mortis conturbat me.

This is all made worse by the cold
for I've no woods and am too old
to comb the beach and haul wreck from the sea.
    Timor mortis conturbat me.

Yet I mind the time, years agone
when the *Maggy* sank with twenty-one
souls and brave big barrels of burgundy.
    Timor mortis conturbat me.

By God's holy grace and a lantern
we saved the barrels and tapped them
filled jugs, poes, hats, all with the sea's red mercy.
    Timor mortis conturbat me.

The smell of the wine, its richness
then troubled us with great sickness.
And not a woman in Welcombe gave pity.
    Timor mortis conturbat me.

Let the wind blow now. I don't care
if kegs of rum, wine, oil appear.
Let Southole thieves grab all. For wreck wrecked me.
    Timor mortis conturbat me.

Next door there's Jim Brock, now dying.
And here, Bill Cottle, he too dying.
We grow up. We grow old. We slither away.
    Timor mortis conturbat me.

This reckless sickle weeds us yearly,
pulls us out as docks from barley
and bends and breaks us with infirmity.
    Timor mortis conturbat me.

It is right nonsense! All of it
fits a crow's hoof. Life's a lost bit
of binder cord wrapped round and round the weather.
    Timor mortis conturbat me.

            1942

Spring's first enthusiasm fades
    into the thick, heavy fruit;
the almond's flamboyant parade
settles down to the tidy nut;
even the cherry's extravagant joke
falls into dowager's ear-rings;
the firm peach and the tight apple
    bend the supple boughs back
to the slackness of autumn.

1942

Spanish Song

Husband!
Kiss me, embrace me. And I'll give you
a clean shirt in the morning.
Never did I see any man alive
look so dead, or pretend
to be asleep when he was wide awake.
Come on, wake up, pull yourself together.
And in the morning I'll give you
a clean shirt.

1942

1943

Poem

In a six-cylinder fury,
Against excessive usury,
Ezra is attacking jewry;
   he forgets the few –
Who've never known what penury
   is, or smelt a Jew.

Qualis the Rothchild, talis Hoare,
Hambro's charge much, the Percys more;
And Grosvenor rents make the poor
   pay back principal
Till they've no interest in the Law
   or the principle

Of breeding men to be paupers,
And killing them off as debtors;
Principle of principal: power:
   milks a cow with calf:
And with finesse, a dead banker
   cuts Jack and Jill in half.

1943

Solitude

I

Oh my God with what agility
does jealousy
              jump into a hot heart
and fit,
      till it fills it,
           or is, a great part.

And how strange it is that I myself
should from myself
              make, riding her thighs
at speed
      (or slow as love needs),
           rivals which are his eyes.

Unfocussed, yet in blindness seeing
all of being;
              opaque, his opal eyes show
sorrow,
      it is as though,
           my wrinkled son had said:
'I who am born was never dead' and said:

'There is no birth, death, joy or sorrow
I am not you,
      nor are you me;
we are each free,
          linked with no separate identity.'

All is as water flowing endlessly
leisurely
          over a smooth hard stone.
Only a thin skin,
          pattern on the water, this, our own.

                                      1943

Dansa
(For Gerald Brennan)
(Poitevin Folk Song, early twelfth century)

I

At the thrust of the stiff spring, oh la,
And to mark joy's swift beginning, oh la,
And stop jealousy's bawling, oh la,
The Queen intends to show
  for whom she is lusting.

  Oh to hell, to hell with the jealous
  May they leave us, and not annoy us,
  Never dance with or amongst us.

II

She's so little and alluring, oh la,
Even the dull sea's dancing, oh la,
And young girls and their men swing
Into this fast dance of spring, oh la.

  Oh to hell, to hell with the jealous
  May they leave us, and not annoy us,
  Never dance with or amongst us.

III

The impotent King's coming, oh la,
To blanket our fiddling, oh la,
For he's afraid some stripling
Will give our Queen's soft yearning, oh la,
  An erect and bold plaything.

  Oh to hell, to hell with the jealous
  May they leave us, and not annoy us,
  Never dance with or amongst us.

IV

But he won't stop our dancing, oh la,
Our Queen's deaf to his bleating, oh la,
She prefers a young sapling, oh la,
Who's adept at caressing
   Our young lady's old longing.

   Oh to hell, to hell with the jealous
   May they leave us, and not annoy us,
   Never dance with or amongst us.

V

Oh, if you'd seen his dancing, oh la,
And his body's tense quivering, oh la,
You'd have said without lying, oh la,
That there was nothing, nothing
   to match our Queen's darling.

   Oh to hell, to hell with the jealous!
   May they leave us, and not annoy us!
   Never dance with or amongst us!

1943

Aubade
(Suggested by the Provencal poem, 'Nereio'
Canto III – Frederic Mistral)

Man

Oh Rose Marie as you are my love
Put your head to the open window
And listen a while to my new song
Sung with sad joy and gay sorrow.

The sky is weeping tears of stars
And the wind has fallen
But the sky will dry its eyes of stars
When the night sees you.

Girl

You move me less than the breeze the branches
My heart is no leaf to your song.
I am going to dive into the deep sea
And become a fish deaf to your song.

Man

Oh Rose Marie if you make yourself
A fish under the deep wave
I will become a fisherman
And will fish for you.

Girl

Oh, but if you then become a fisherman
I will break your net with my wings
For I will then fly into the clear sky
And become a bird deaf to your song.

Man

Oh Rose Marie if you make yourself
A bird above the green fields
I will become a bird hunter
And will hunt you.

Girl

Yes, but if you become a bird hunter
You will not catch me in your snare
For I will land and become white clover
Lost in a field deaf to your song.

Man

Oh Rose Marie if you make yourself
A grass in the thick meadow
I will become a shower of rain
And will fall on you.

Girl

Yes, but if you become a shower of rain
You will not touch me with your drops
For I will become a cloud above you
And drift to a land deaf to your song.

Man

Oh Rose Marie if you make yourself
A cloud drifting to India
I will become the lusty wind
And carry you.

Girl

Very well, but if you become a gust of wind
You will not move me with your breeze
For I'll dissolve into the sun's warm rays
And melt the strings of your guitar.

Man

Oh Rose Marie if you make yourself
A ray of the lovely sun
I will become a green lizard
And will drink you.

Girl

Even if you become a salamander
You will not drink me with your lust
For I will become a mysterious moon
Lighting a witch cursing your song.

Man

Oh Rose Marie if you make yourself
As naked and smooth as the moon
I will become the softest mist
And cover you.

Girl

Well, even if you become a mist
You will cover the moon not me
For I will become a virginal rose
Untouched by your passionate song.

Man

Oh Rose Marie if you make yourself
As open and free as the rose
I will become as the heavy dew
And lie on you.

Girl

Go! Lover! Go! and be off with you
Never! Never! will you have me
For I will become a gnarled old oak tree
And let the owls out-hoot your song.

Man

Oh Rose Marie if you make yourself
As patient and still as a tree
I will become climbing ivy
And embrace you.

Girl

And then let me tell you your arms will hold
Wood only wood, for to spite you
I will become a nun of St. Blas
And let the Mass silence your song.

Man

Oh Rose Marie if you make yourself
As innocent as a white nun
I will become a chaplain
And confess you.

Girl

And if you pass the doors of the convent
You'll find all the nuns around me
For I'll be lying in a winding sheet
Dead and the dead are deaf to song.

Man

Oh Rose Marie if you make yourself
As yielding as a poor corpse
I will become the loving earth
And thus have you.

Girl

Now at last I begin to believe you
And can see you are not joking
Here is my ring, and my door is open
The key to my heart is your song.

Man

Oh Rose Marie you lift me from the dead
And look since seeing you
Only the stars, my Rose Marie,
Only they have fled.

1943

Ballad of Stratton Gaol

Great souls in prison cells
lie
and commit no perjury
but to themselves do injury,
farming their mind's boundless demesne
for a harvest of fears, dreams and worry.
To their sorrow, pain comes as a relief,
Pain comes as mercy to the confined saint and common
    thief.

There's my friend Gandhi
who
prays and spins, then spins and prays,
patiently passing endless days,
a man no Empire could dismay
nor he an Empire or himself betray,
for under his leathern skin he too holds a prisoner:
his proud spirit which, humbled, is his power.

And then dear Mauberley,
where
he is I do not know, but fear
for him, for he knew no fear
nor unlike many did he disappear
to Canada with Europe's chaos near.
Where he had made his home, he stayed in loyalty,
spoke out his mind to be accused of treachery.

God, what an age is this
when
prisons are improvised and filled
before they're built. Those who are killed
get off with half the captive's addled
safety. For one it's blood, the other tears are spilled.
It's all the same to us – 'Pro bono patria.'
Let's place all double beds in storage for Utopia!

There was a couple
who
lived where I was living;
She waters her garden, biting
her nails, waiting, looking and waiting
for the post from the prisoner who's pining
for news of the girl who's waiting – which may sound pathos
but is for all that true, and to their dance sheer damn loss.

Where do I come in?
I am.
For what? For salving from the sea
thirty gallons of petrol – for me!
And using same for purposes of husbandry.
Poor husbandry! Poor me! Both wedded to poverty!
Now my cows unmilked; some stacks open; some corn
    uncarried.
Here I am by four white-washed walls confined, no little
    worried.

But I am not alone,
a fly
shares my captivity, and he

shares my restlessness for home and he,
like my mind, flits endlessly and fruitlessly,
both of us passengers to the same futility.
But between the fly and I is this disparity:
In weight; we share the same fixed gravity.

Stratton Gaol 1943

Summer

What is Summer?
   The sun's stride through the wide
                             cornfields
   Combing its fingers over the ripening prawn of barley?
   Or does it hide in the
                  tiny coral pimpernel,
   The lanky foxglove or hedge of honeysuckle,
   In scent of rose or fragrant jasmine?
Is Summer the blue pavilion
   apple branch burdened or strawberry plant
                             bejewelled?

1943

Jasmine lies as gently on the evening air
Or water spiders tread as lightly as these tiny hands which are
Now cast like shells upon the surf of sleep.
And where is there any petal as delicate as this eyelid
To enclose all the innocence of a rose?
How then could I teach him?
And more important what? The answer is:
Nothing. More than this poet knows now lies within this cot.

Should I not rather be taught by him, to learn
How all things are toys to be thrown upon the floor
And to value feelings above any article;
Keeping affections, in spite of their consequence or
Effect; oblivious to the ultimate
Released within the immediate; to perceive
Loneliness as a state of being one
Yet apart in entirety, though still contained as he is within his
   mother's heart?

   1943

Song

I am kneeling in the chapel of Saint Simon,
Left by the tide of time to kneel alone.
My love's taken, and my heart is broken.

I am sitting in the chapel before the altar
Left alone by the tide turning all to winter.
My love's taken, and my heart is broken.

Leaving me alone the tide has turned and gone
And night now dives to rescue the drowning sun.
My love's taken, and my heart is broken

And the drowning sun is drenching my last summer
And I too will die and go to my dead lover.
My love's taken, and my heart is broken

Now the drowning sun burns on the thin horizon
I will drown in the waves, in the tide. It is all done.
My love's taken, and my heart is broken.

   1943

1944

For A Young Man, Aged 90

At Windsor where the castle keep
Watches the quiet village half asleep
On banks by which deep waters sweep
Where the tired willows bend and weep

With graceful grief their sorrows hide
In their own shade, in their leaf's pride,
Which like child's fingers in the water slide
Following the flow of the great river's tide.

There where the old College sprawls
Over the village with its fields and halls
Was born within four modest walls
A child. He had his life but that was all.

No wealth, nor talent to be great
Was his, his whole estate
He held within his hands, the weight
Nothing. – His hands were his estate.

His eyes his tutor. As he played
He helped his uncle as he made
The sharp-nosed boats, the oar's fine blade.
Holding these tools, he learned a trade.

And by canals where barges push
Their heavy way and leave their wash,
And where the dragon-fly still flash
And the fat trout rise and fall and splash

There where the wooden lock-gates creak
And old punts lie too full to leak
And vicious pike their quarry seek
Under the roots of a dusty creek,

A boy did sleep, a man did wake
For he had dreamed and dreams can make
What they will of us. They take
Us in the head till our hearts break

With following. For him no more
The little boat, the varnished oar;
For him, the railway shed and store,
The cleaner's rag, the fire box roar.

At Nine Elms he did 'his shunting'.
Then drove the non-stop down to Reading
From Waterloo, seldom missing
A minute. His engine shining.

Saving his Company's coal from waste
By thorough stoking, and that slow haste
'Which needs no brakes – or what is worse
Buffers!' – Though none of that, his cost!

It was his character to save
Fuel. The only man he called a knave
Was a bad fireman; and he'd slave
To make the loss up, and then forgave

His mate. For 60 years he kept
His large family and his prompt
Engine burnished like brass and swept.
And pensioned off, he left her and he wept

And went home to his small garden,
An old sad man unbroken
Feeling his engine was forsaken
To bad drivers, and its buffers broken.

Sometimes he would sing in sadness
Songs of his boyhood and gladness;
His family watching his distress;
His grandchild noting how verse compressed.

He who endures this life a year
Drinks his own weight in his own tears.
And this man's 90 and no tear
stains the old cheek of his young years.

Again he sits by a great river
Watching the small boats that never
Leave the cool comfort of the river.
And like this, I pray, he'll sit for ever.

22 June 1944

The Crone's Lament
(Translated from the Spanish)

Oh, I wish I were an orange tree,
For if I were, my breasts would be
Round as the fruit on the orange tree.
Then Time would take no toll of me
Nor my lover see this change in me
And forever more his hand could pluck
Fresh, firm fruit from a gnarled old tree.

And if he were a banana tree
Just think how useful that would be
Spring would see him growing towards me;

All Summer shew him rising to me;
Autumn would be our yielding;
And winter only our withdrawing –
If my love were a banana tree.

1944

Air Raid

Like skulls with all their fears still there
The houses squat around the square,
And through their broken windows stare
Into each other, with fixed despair.

In the hall of No. 21
Where my aunt received anyone who was somebody,
A white glove like a severed hand lies on the floor.
Her 'phone rings; but nobody answers her trunk call from Hades
To tell Stone where Mr Ronald sits
At dinner – between two corsaged, safe ladies.

Now rats are residents at Embassies,
Cockroaches call, and mice are prodigal:
This war does more than spoil her Season
It's quite upset her Peke's poor reason.

And now the drunken staircase climbs the peeling walls
Into the salon where bats bleat madrigals.
Across the hearth two marble cupids sprawl.
Dust settles quietly, inheriting it all.

1944

Strophe and Anti-Strophe at Bakerloo

With the vision of the blind
   I see the neap-tide of spring
Move in its deep
   groin of sleep
   till as a powered wave it flings its spray
Onto the rocks, then ebbs, then falls away,
   leaving its fleece of flowers
As lilac or as lavender behind,
   then as heather or as ling
The fingering surf of spring creeps
     to an old wall where as wisteria it weeps tears
   of mauve disarray
For the wind to tidy all away
   as the rain shears this fleece of flowers
with the clumsiness of thunder showers.

With the vision of the blind I see
But cannot see,
   for up and down this city street
I walk on tired tethered feet
   and with a sad persistent tread
Follow the crowds of the unburied dead
Into the Tube's anatomy
As it devours me
   into the soiled sweat and heat
Till I'm digested as soiled meat
   and packed within its bowels I'm led
Through busy labyrinths of the dead

With the vision of the blind I see
   the earth excited with leaf and with labour
There,
     where
         the plough turns the furrow

And the belly of my fields lie fit for the harrow
    and the lumbersome corn drill parades
And the seed falls back to its secrecy
    and in blind need gives brief succour
To the earth which thirsts for
    that which is all hunger.
    Are our small eyes so shallow
Because our hearts are fallow?
    Oh! whose hand can hold the spade
And sow our eyes into each others' hearts again
    till the ghost we are, is laid?

With all the callousness of fixed despair
We with marked indifference stare
    at the bunks where the bombed-out keep
Their rags of dreams in soiled sleep.
    And on a bench a couple lie quite dead,
I lift my hat. The lovers move. It was ecstasy instead ...
A faux pas; pardonable; compare
Love with death and there
    is little difference as they creep
Into the grave or bed of sleep.

                                                  1944

Mi Pensamiento
(Translated from the Spanish)

My heart burns away slowly
Its smoke sears my eyes.
At your step it burns fiercely.
Desire clarifies.

With the slow eyes of the soul
I gaze at you
With the quick eyes of the mind
I dissemble.

My patience is finished
Pretence has died.
When with just looking at you
I was satisfied.

1944

The Mason's Epitaph

He was neither prince nor politician,
no priest and no poet,
as the world knows them; but he was the man
to smooth stones, make each fit

straight to his quoin, and thus used less mortar
than contract masons waste,
with the next job as their present master,
in their slow toil of haste.

He worked no fixed hours, he just came and went,
carrying a jug of cold tea;
he'd stay till he'd used up all his cement,
then leave, with no temerity.

His work was such that each action contained
its own contemplation;
the more he gave his work, the more he gained
in strict meditation

on stones of infinite shape. He weighed
their neat rigidity.
Disciplined by working with these, he made
his own philosophy

which was as sound as any Analects,
– at least, in application –
all men and things to their own nature fit
with or without salvation.

'Larch is no good for a lintel,' he said,
'it warps young and rots old
true to its nature; and from friends,' he said,
'expect from friends their colds.'

Protected by these exact measurements
he spent his evenings home.
Freed from resentments and disappointment,
married – to be alone.

His wife, a woman of monotonous lust,
without one attraction.
He kept her pregnant, for he knew this must
assure some relaxation.

But to assess his solid character,
words do not weigh enough.
Observe his walls, they maintain his nature;
see where he smoothed the rough

and how his beam's morticed. Then you will see
that civilization
exists where men work for posterity
and build from sheer passion

for durability. Prust built that way;
this shippen here proves it.
Living, he gave us this, and now we say:
He died to no profit.

                                           1944

Flotsam

Christ, is this Thy Cross, tossed
by a wave at my feet, complete
morticed and set and wet
with a blunt nail through the white deal wood?
Made in a hurry and thrown on to some poor fellow's pillow
lifting and enveloping.
If Thy Cross, Christ, can in spite night's
storm and day's tempest ride tide,
the gale's lust and the sleet, and keep
an unknown appointment so punctually, surely
I should find You more easily, especially
as You lie in my heart like a green leaf in an old book
revealed, if only I could find my heart, open it, and look?

1944

Dartmoor

Where waves of earth
   Have sprays of stone
And break with granite
   And fling heather foam

Over the tors
   Which stand and shed
Beams of thick darkness
   To mislead the dead,

Who with full sails
  Of shadow steer
Over this ocean
  With its tide of fear.

Here lonely farms
  With noisy sheep
Support poor peasants
  With all but sleep.

His haggard cows
  Graze bracken fields;
They display much horn;
He conceals their yield.

The broken hedge
  Once walled with stone
Defines a dwelling
  More prison than home.

1944

The Mongrel

I

Does the terror of the tiger's tooth
  Tear through a horse's dream?
And the fierce heat of a forest fire
  Still burn within the panther's quiet brain
As with cautious paw it treads the night
Remembering the soft embers' cruel pain?

What forgotten spite does the slow viper
  So suddenly recall
As it wakes, and makes its terrible revenge?
  And does the timid deer it bites redeem

With its eye's gentleness, the mammoth's clumsiness which,
    trumpeting in panic,
Trod upon the first snake that, sleeping, slept uncursed by heavy
    dreams?

Must the assiduous spider forever spin,
    And Arachne's curse never be undone?
Must her blind fingers never cease from weaving
    Till all the world is woven in her web,
And the wind is held by frail sails of silken industry
And is embalmed by what it broke so ruthlessly?

What slow torture do the blind roots suffer
    When they writhe and twist around one another,
And break out from the bank like a broken hand,
    Still clutching the indifferent earth
As our mind, our dreams when we awaken,
As our mouth, the breast at the moment of our birth?

II

What is our life but a slow remembering?
    What is our death but a quick forgetting?
But forgetting does not mean that the memory is erased,
    Nor can death break what cannot be broken.
Though lonely, we are not separate;
And though we may forget, nothing can be forgotten.

Yes, I remember. Now I am remembering.
    When I was a child – that is, the last time I was a child –
Oh, do not ask me who I am,
    For only by remembering am I becoming.
And by becoming, to exist which is – no, it is not to be,
But to be not; and in that negation His affirmation, our
    resurrection.

Which is as easily said as it's forgotten, as I've forgotten.
    What was I saying? I was saying
When I was a child my dreams were so real
    I thought I had lived them; and as experiences told them to my
        friends.

They said: I was lying. But I was not lying.
It was that I could not distinguish between what I had
    experienced and what I had only dreamed.

Then as I grew up (from or to? – we need not argue),
  I found myself remembering experiences I had never
    experienced
And dreams I had never dreamt,
  None of which worried me, till they, pitying me, worried me.
'Poor boy!' they used to say:
'He is cursed with weak legs and a strong imagination.'

So, as a consequence, I became strangely proficient at football
  And would pray: 'Dear God, let me sleep but do not wake me
    into dreams.'
But to no avail – prayers seldom are;
  I suppose their value lies not as the means to obtain
But in the request *per se* – which is, I agree, quite by the way
– A beggar by the way! What am I talking about?

What beggar? By which way? What do those words make me
    remember?
  Dare I remember? It was uphill; He looked hot; it was heavy.
He spat at Him. Who did? Oh, do not ask me who I am,
  For I do not know or I dare not remember,
As I live recalling lives I have not lived
And die forgetting the death I dare not remember.

Yes, this is all very muddled and all very mystic.
  Poor boy et cetera running after his imagination with weak
    legs.
But can we imagine or is it we remember?
  A son sometimes finishes a deceased father's sentence
In the same hand. But whose hand?
True, shorthand is one of the advantages of poetry.

You follow? But who leads? And how can I answer
  If you do not question? Must I frame the question
Then the answer – picking my words on the way, begging my
    way?
  It is as though I were working at the coal face

70

In a mine closed, sealed many years ago.
Not very encouraging. The mute worm calls to his deaf mate in
    the tight earth; –

Not very encouraging. No wonder you cannot tell whether it is
    coming or going
    Or which end its tail is ... As I was saying, only I will keep
        interrupting;
When I was a child I dreamt my father's fears:
    'No one knows through what wild age roams back the rose',
And as I matured to memory, forgetting my own life, I
    remembered theirs,
My ancestors, understudies, princes and beggars by the way.

They stand in a queue stretching behind me and before me,
    All with the same features and weak legs et cetera ...
Projections and extensions of the I – but whose eye?
    It is apparent that each man is his own father;
And his son, too. No wonder you cannot tell whether I am
    coming or going
Or whether I'm imagining or whether I am remembering.

III

The present is where we are. But where are we?
    You may just as well try and pin the weaving swallow to the
        wall.
History is a diary I mislaid; tradition, the residuum of
    experience;
    Or, as Ez would say: 'What works or whatever' and we might
        add:
It is a resolution I made, forgot and remembered on the way.
He spat at Him. But who did? Oh, do not ask me who I am.

In what degree does the daffodil alter
    The same yellow trumpet as spring shuffles in
Somewhat diffidently, rather like a ham actor who knows his
    lines have all become platitudes.
Mais il y avait une fois, c'était une rose noire
Elle ne fleurit pas dans un petit jardin
Mais dedans l'esprit d'un poète qui avait les jambes – Hélas! ...

And a mind which is all parenthesis
    Far too impatient to punctuate
As, like blindness blindfolded, it begs for light
    To illumine the black rose which was so white
Before we let His blood and it stained it with night
And we crowned ourselves with thorns, monarchs of mortality,

Emperors of a grave, imprisoned in our personality
    Judged by our bones and jailed in our flesh.
Is there no way but that way, so rough, so steep, so heavy? . . .
    Or can we, by remembering our millennium of past
Or by imagining our untrodden future, escape that state
Where we all reign free as kings, yet subject – subject for a
    comedy. –

But not very amusing; not in the best of taste –
    What with time tied to our tail, teasing us,
As we attempt the tightrope and step from the narrow womb
    into the narrow grave,
    Immortal – as the cigar we burned into the carpet.
Must this roundabout revolve and this pattern persist and never
    alter?
Well? . . . I'm sorry, I was forgetting. Having put the question I
    must also find the answer.

'Yes, do. And give me a ring sometime. I must be going. . . .'
'So soon? Good-bye! As I was saying, must this roundabout . . .'
    'What, back again? Forgotten anything?'
'My breast. It's possible I might need it.' 'Where did you put it?'
    'It is in your hand.'
'I beg your pardon. And so heavy too . . . Do let me post it . . .'
Such is the marriage of our minds that every whore is chaste
And every wife's a spinster. No, that is not the way –

For though we go uphill and come we never can arrive.
    Made in his image? Perhaps, at any rate in desperation we clasp
    her to ourselves
And from that brief oblivion wake holding a woman; the god
    escapes our paw;
    And we are left as lonely as we were before,
Having tasted of our death from which we clumsily withdraw,
Having reproduced ourselves, ourselves and nothing more.

But sometimes in moments of absent-mindedness I have
  remembered
  Lives I have lived and deaths I have not died.
No, I am not thinking of instinct: the serpent's spite, the
  panther's caution,
  Spider assiduous, or the stallion's proud fear –
As it stands a miracle of grace with powered flanks and muscles
  laced,
Thunder in its hoofs and lightning in its eye.

Is there a solitude which is not loneliness?
  And somewhere someone's company which is not interruption
Of a meditation (mere observation or introspection)?
  Is there a love which is liberation?
For our intimacy is all desperation
For self-expression, self-oblivion.

Is there nowhere where dust does not fall through the air
  Closing Helen's eyes? I am sick. I must die. Lord . . .
'*DAMAROIDS will give you new life.*' '*All change for Charing
  Cross.*'
  You see what I mean? What was I saying?
'You were talking about some girl called Helen,
Wasn't she the dame who rode through Paris naked on a
  horse?'

Why, yes, of course. And the time will come when Jesus Christ
  will be
  One of Robin Hood's good men. And his manger lie
In an adjoining room to Nephertiti's golden spoon.
  For further reference see 'Myths Ancient and Modern'.
'*How interesting! Now I know why they're called hot cross
  buns. . . .*'
No, I'm not thinking of instinct. In a blind world of grass
  The old ewes graze. (Do sheep count sheep
To get to sleep? Or is it all sleep?)
  The ewe fattens on the grass; the grass fattens on the ewe,
A self-contained, self-sufficient: mutton oblivion.
The daffodil may not differ. But insentience is not to be.

But to be not. No, I'm not talking of instinct: blood oblivion.
   We cannot fulfil our destiny by denying our destiny,
Nor reach our destination by staying precisely where we are.
   And where are we? For my part, at the station to which I have
      hurried,
My ticket in my mouth, my coat tails flying . . .
   Frantically I accost a porter: 'Which is my train?' I ask.

'Just where are you going?' 'To death! To death!' I shout.
   He looks at my ticket. 'Why mate,' he grins, 'that's where you
      are.' –
Not very encouraging. And I daresay if I were a guide at the
      Hampton Court maze,
   It would soon be cluttered with skeletons
Who had lost their way following my way,
Not the way I forgot but the way I dare not remember.

But sometimes when I sleep, the tide of time seems to recede
   And leaves me as permanent as a star – but what's as lonely as
      a star?
Or a man's mind drifting in the ocean of the night?
   And it is all night, though dreams deceive us and light blinds us;
It is all night. And we are lost; we have not only forgotten our
      destination
But mislaid ourselves as well – whom we now seek in a sort of
      frantic blindman's buff,

As though ourselves could be our destination
   Or finding it the slightest consolation,
As if such rags of spirit patched with pride were ever 'raiment for
      a soul'.
   Are we deluded, or self-deluded? Are we forgotten,
Or have we forgotten? And were we to remember
Would we not be remembered?

Precisely. All our conversations are soliloquies.
   We are talking in each other's sleep. Not very encouraging.
No wonder this poem is so inarticulate,
   And you cannot tell whether you are coming or I'm going.
No, it is not that I have nothing to communicate
But that nobody will lift the receiver off the telephone

As it rings in an empty room, an agony of privacy,
    Reductio ad absurdam of self-expression;
No wonder I, as a young man fall into the habits of an old man
    Finding myself walking round and round Leicester Square
(Yes, a peg, etc.) talking to myself, quite forgetting the question,
    never remembering the answer,
Observing a pigeon alight, perch, and then belime Shakespeare's
    stone bald head.

'To buried merit raise the tardy bust'...
    And to living Grace we improvise a cross,
Which irrelevant association brings me back to the point of my
    departure.
    Now up and down the street I run on urgent feet;
It is not that I evade but that He will pursue
And in each face find more cause for pity

Than I have compassion, and so hate them for my inadequacy
    As all flee from me as I from Him
Through the arches of the years wading in my unshed tears.
    Oh, do not ask me who I am, for I would forget
What I dare not remember, running from my memory with tired
    legs
With His mercy like an unclaimed mongrel following, still
    following.

Round and round the lives I've lived, in and out the deaths I have
    not died,
    And the more I kick Him the closer to my heel He lies
And the more terrible the tenderness of His eyes
    Which I recall but will not recognize
And must deny, for were I to admit Him
He would devour my heart and leave me with no part
    of it,

Not even the weight or stain of it –
    And so I throw the dog a bone and tell him to go home,
And turn from that memory which can only be imagined
    And from that phantom which walks and haunts my mind,
For it is not possible, is it, say,
That I watched Him, the beggar in my way

And spat at Him, as He went on His way,
   It is not possible, is it, say –
Yet how do you, or you, explain that as a child
   Before I cried my mother's name I wept for this,
And whoever's tears they were, it was my shame
With every detail nailed into my mind?

It is not possible, is it possible?
   For since our features, gestures, weak legs, etc.
Can be handed down the indifferent years
   Cannot experiences and memories also
Be inherited and suddenly remembered
And then forgotten once again?

Who has not felt some time or other
   That they had been there before where they could never have
     been before
And to their own surprise see
   Their quick hand find the secret of the door?
So I am haunted by deaths I have not died
Till I become a ghost haunting my own life;

For as the fierce heat of the forest fire still burns
   Within the panther's quiet brain,
So can I, in moments of absent-mindedness, involuntarily recall
   That brief look of pity and the everlasting shame
And run from Him as all men run from me,
Fleeing from each birth, running to each death,

Trying to forget, dreading to remember,
   Pretending to seek what I am determined not to find,
As blind bats cling to their element of night
   So I my disbelief; for doubt is all my faith and darkness is my
     light,
So let the black rose bleed till it is white,
I will deny my eyes that see beyond their sight,

And watch the reckless cavalry of waves
   Ride with their white manes flying,
And how they charge with lifted lance,
   Then on the beach are broken lying

In a fret of surf till the tide recedes
And they form their futile ranks again.

As the blind moon – is it the blind moon that beckons?...
  'What? – *Your shoe-lace is undone.*'

                                                    1944

1945

The Single Eye

For Gerald Brenan

They say that man is blessed with sight.
They are wrong! They are wrong!

They say his soul speaks through his eyes.
He is dumb! He is dumb!

The seeing eye is for wanton boys
For the young! for the young!

The grown man's eyes are blind with lies
Yet he has one, he has one

Which blind to sight sees through the night
To the sun! To the sun!

The grown man's had but a single eye
Since time began, since time began!

The blind man's eye like a serpent lies
And passionate his tongue, his tongue!

The dreaming man sees with this waking eye
As it rises to the sun! The sun!

The rising eye is through the thighs of night
And it is strong! It is strong.

And the sleeping man with his two blind eyes
Sees beyond sight as his serpent tries
To spit into the sun! The sun!

August 1945

Impromptu For A Child

Like little clouds on a green sky, my sheep
Graze within their innocence of sleep;

With powered flanks my arab horse
Burns like a hill of autumn gorse;

And down the lane the slow cows pass
From dreams of hay to dreams of grass.

This Earth has feet, here clay can walk,
The old elms speak, their blind leaves talk.

1945

Briony

Like a waterfall of wind
Her hair falls to her shoulder
Fair? Oh, nothing is so fair
As this hair which curls in laughter

Round my hand, as light as light
Lies on the skin of water.
Where is there anything so fine?
There, where the heather spider

Spins from the night's anatomy
A web to catch the stars
Which dawn lets fall as dew
As it mounts the sun, the tiger,

And through the blue pavilion
Rides where the honeysuckle spills
Its heavy secret scent
Into an evening indolent

And tired from picking passion fruit
And tying up the vines
Before the grapes' full lust
Bursts into black wine.

But there is no web woven
Nor head of lovely hair to hold
Time back from his pursuit
Or tether the mad equipage, age

Which tramples into dust
With its wrinkles and its rust
And its violence and its lust.
Dear Jesus, watch this child for me:
In loving her, I love Thee.

1945

Moto Perpetuo

And this evening, as the sun
Emblazons the horizon
And lifts the leaves with yellow light,
The frail antennae of slow night,
Then sinks; and severs the sad ocean
With the forearm of its might,
Making my eyes bleed – for beauty
Is the quick agony of this sight

Of this evening, as the sea
Sullen, bruised and angry
Sulks; then strikes with flails of spray
For the insane wind to blow away
Over the gaunt cliffs to the trees'
Leaflessness, shorn, torn, disarray.
Then the tide turns and the gale gives,
Cedes, recedes taking its wrath of spray

From this evening, now so mild
It lies down to sleep like a child
Dropping its toys of wantonness
Instantly into deep sleep's steepness
Where it is reconciled
To night, and its first nothingness,
Where with a linnet's lightness it lies
Safe, where the panther purrs with his eyes so wild

Into the night, as the lake
With silken skin slides as a snake
Under the shadow's velvet train,
Heavy with tears and soaked with pain.
Sorrow is what the sun forsakes;
And night, the anatomy of pain,
Benumbs our restlessness with sleep
In which we dream of the sun, then wake

To this morning, as the light
Listlessly lifts the lid of night,
And the fat hips of the ocean
Swing into the harbour, as a woman
Walking before a sailor might
Slap her great thighs of waves upon
The jetty's wall to the spray's delight ...

1945

Practical Ballads

I

The site: choose a dry site.
Avoid building against a bank.
Leaning a building to a bank may save putting up a wall,
but dampness will seep through,
you'll see your mortar sweat,
you'll be feeding to keep your pig warm,
this way she'll not fatten, profitably;
you may get roast out of it, but no bacon.

The size: Floor eight foot by eight foot good –
and slope off to a gutter;
pig's urine swells the bean pods; cover from flies.
Height: that is your problem, your comfort,
for it is you who have to get in and fling the dung out,
at least once a week, this is most important.

Now is the time to be generous:
Throw the straw in, not one wad, but two, three, four –
The more straw the more dung
The more dung the more straw, eventually.
Oh, cover the pig she'll trample it.

As to the door, observe the stable and copy that;
Make it of seasoned wood that won't warp as mine did.
Don't buy a bolt get a smith to make one –
Strength, not ornament, is necessary.
And that goes for a pig-sty, and poetry.

1945

II

Some people don't like the rain. I like the rain.
I stand at the door watching it plop my pails full
thinking: it is doing my work for me;
now I shan't have to carry from the well this evening;
it is washing the lime in on East Hill;
The pig dung I spread for the barley, it is washing that in too;
Young grass will come sooner,
calves do better.
I cannot say I prayed for this rain.
But I wished for it.
And there's the wind driving it up the valley
it falls like the skirt of a dancer.

1945

To Plough

In a blind world of grass
The horse takes all reality
Between his teeth, his tail
Rhythmically records tranquillity.

In water's sensuous complete caress
The lazy trout serenely swims
To where the oak's rheumatic roots
Grip the pool beneath its brim.

And there dissolved in shagreen light
Like new cut pewter with the sun upon
Its skin, it sleeps into the lake of night
Within its wet endymion.

And from the earth's renewing lust
My rusty ploughshare takes its shine
Riding the furrow and the year
Taking its pleasure from the thighs of time.

Into the silent sky's blue fountain of white light
The alert lark lifts and rising
Falls into its element of air
And for the thirsty sun it spills
An avalanche of liquid notes.

The patient earthworm leavening the soil
The wood louse in its wilderness of bark
The fig tree propped against an old cob wall
All meditate within, and in their element exist,
And being so, are eyes for the blind earth, and thus
Stare back into the vision and see the sight of God.

1945

Notes of a Dream

The thick blood of my heart
has fallen out
and my feet are full of it.

Who'll follow a drunk lizard into the sand?
I've mounted his back,
and he rides me well:
Look! how he follows;
fast I race after him.
The lizard and I are together again:
I rip his white belly with my nails, and bleed.

1945

Lines Written for a Wine Merchant's Christmas Card

Old bottles on an old shelf contain
The sun's exuberance slaked with rain,
And in dusty stillness hold
The grape's vivaciousness
That laughed in scarlet or wept in gold,
Under the wooden press
Of autumn's wantonness.
So much into so little is all at last resolved:
The grape in wine finds rest
And man to dust is pressed.
Before this Feast, there was His sacrifice.
Before this Peace, there was their pain.
From their bloodshed must only wine remain.
But these lines cannot express their loss
For words have not wine's dumb loquaciousness.

1945

Carol
(Adapted from the fifteenth century,
author unknown)

This song's to a girl;
It's to her
Whom Jesus Christ chose
For His Mother.

He was as gentle
In repose
As dew in April
Lies in the rose.

He was as gentle
As His birth
As dew in April
touches the earth.

He was as gentle
At her breast
As dew in April
Falls to its rest.

There has never been
Any other
more fitted to be
Jesus's Mother.

1945

1946

Appenato
(for Kathleen Ferrier)

Eurydice:
Oh my love, I am as lonely
As a lost river flowing
Through a desert slowly
To a sea receding
With its tide withdrawing
And its waves unyielding.

Orpheus:
Oh my love, to be lonely
Is like death only sleepless
For as a dream I am seeking
A dreamer who is restless
And thus, unless you sleep to receive me,
or wake to my dream of thee,
I, as a ghost must forever haunt my own loneliness,
Oh Eurydice, Eurydice.

1946

Drinking Song

Drink! For the night is flowing like black wine,
And drowns our wasted lives with our spilt time,
And floods the deserts till they, like lakes,
Support the stars in a lost design.
   O! The only hour worth living
     Is now! Is now! Is now!

Drink! For our time is flowing with the night
And life is short except where wine sheds light
Upon us as we swim beneath our dreams,
Grovelling for the relics of delight.
   O! The only cup worth filling
     Is this! Is this! Is this!

Drink! For the grape is full of wantonness,
Like an Arab girl whose nakedness
Has given the sun, its quietus;
Within her breasts voluptuousness.
   O! The only girl worth having
     Is wine! Is wine! Is wine!

Drink! For the thirsty tongue was made to taste
Both wine and women before they waste
Into the grave's sobriety, and there
Lie forever immoderately chaste!
   O! The only wine worth drinking
     Is love! Is love! Is love!

                                                  1946

1947

Ascension

It was not that I raised myself to Him
But that He reached down for me.
And during that time, after they had found the tomb empty,
I was among them.
Seeing me, Mary Magdalene embraced me.
'Do not cling to me thus,' I cried
'While I am still a man.'
'What a man loves, he does become.'
For two days, I wept at her grief for me.
For two days I walked beside her
sharing no burden, casting no shadow.
It was not that I had risen from the dead
but love had not died in me.

Then, as I watched them disperse
back to the nets, the loom, and the last
from which I'd called them,
I saw their disappointment that the Kingdom I had brought,
had not been the Kingdom they had sought,
The only crown I wore,
Scratched my forehead badly;
The only throne I knew,
Pattered on four little hooves.
And as I watched them and walked with them I wondered

whether I had not sinned greatly:
by burdening their innocence with a vision they couldn't share;
by confusing them, setting father against son, son against father.

I stood for a moment observing Peter
dexterously mending the mesh in his net,
And in that moment I saw the whole tapestry of tears
which I had woven:
Two thousand years, with less love at the end of it;
And I saw Charity's long crusade of savagery;
Tolerance turning to bigotry and faith to the thumbscrew.
And seeing all this and foreseeing all that
With so few, so few, not even twelve to understand,
I walked on, leaving no footprints save in my remorse.
The earth I loved had hands.
It held me by the feet.

Then in the garden, that garden, I suffered a second agony;
their nails, gentle to these nails,
their cross light to this cross: the realization
That I should not have projected the struggle within me
but should have lived it internally:
denied myself, betrayed myself, judged myself and thus given man
that love he could not give me: a compassion
beyond the Passion.
That was the thought which crucified me.
Forgive me, for I knew what I had done.

It was not that I raised myself to Him
but that He, in great mercy, reached down for me.

1947

1948

Epitaph on an Unknown Passenger

Having descended the escalator at Queensway Tube Station
and walking towards the platform on my way to Leicester
   Square,
I heard a man running up behind me,
as if he were being pursued,
or was racing to catch the last train:
which was odd, since it was during the morning.
He caught up with me just as I was turning a corner:
his coat tails flying,
his spectacles falling to the ground.
'Excuse me,' he cried as he passed me, 'excuse me,'
and he ran on to the platform.
And there I saw him fling himself in front of the train
as it emerged from the tunnel.
As they dragged his corpse from the line
I wondered what sort of man this was
who, while chucking his life away,
had clung on to his good manners.

                                                  1948

1949

(Written on the fly leaf of a book for a young lady who asked
for an indiscreet inscription to put under her pillow)

To her whose eyes are eloquent
                              since she,
   finding a better purpose for her lips,
Taught them to speak,
            so wantonly.

To her whose lips have sight
                              since she,
   pitying mine which sought hers blindly,
Taught her own to see,
            yet modestly.

To her whose tongue is nimble
                              since she,
   being willing to suggest but not invite,
Taught it to imitate –
            well, figuratively...

To her whose mouth's secret which reveals her thighs' red rose,
   and that I,
would kiss and enter and with him to gallop after would
Teach those eyes my answer
Teach her eyes to close,
   and that – quite literally!

                              April 1949

Song

Larks are the sparks
   Torn from the revolving earth
As it turns like a wheel through the night.

Larks are the sound
   To which silence is echo:
From their throat flows the river of light.

Larks are the dance
   In which the dancer is still –
Finding the perfect pose for their restless will.

Larks are the form
   To which all movement moves,
Sculpture bends, and music sings.
   They have such grace they fly from us;
   They are God's grace with wings!

29 December 1949

1950

A Ballad

Oh shall I sing of Josephine?
She was a maiden of eighteen
Betrothed to one called Edward Stone
Whom she did love and loved alone.

Now just before their wedding day
When the sun slept on the new mown hay
Poor Edward Stone fell ill and died
While Josephine knelt by his side.

Bewildered by her brief she went
Into grief's lonely banishment
And though her friends consoled, she wept
And weeping stood where he still slept.

For seven years she never said
A single word or raised her head;
The village thought she'd lost her tongue.
When Josephine burst into song.

Now would you hear what Josephine
Sang to the village on the green?
*'If it's true love cannot die
Edward still lives as well as I'*

And straightway to her home she ran
Hand in hand with a phantom man
For whom she baked a little pie
Since ghosts must eat or they must die.

Now laughing like a happy bride
She lives with Edward at her side
She never quarrels with this ghost
And loving him, her love's not lost.

1950

Canon For Three Critics

I'm as blind as a bat,
   Therefore just the man
To evaluate Moore and Picasso.
And looking at Epstein, I see
   No good or evil.

                    We are three critics, we
                    Judge Art for its validity.

I'm as deaf as a post.
   Therefore I'm able
To write about Britten's Concerto
And listening to Webern I hear
   Nothing remarkable.

                    We are three critics, we
                    Judge Art for its validity.

I'm as dumb as I look
   Therefore a critic
Who reviews what you do but I cannot;
What is fashionable I commend:
   What is not: is not.

1950

Oh rose of sorrow
Which blooms with my regret,
   Shew mercy to my memory;
Fade: let me forget.

1950

There was a man
   who collected kindness;
His cupboard was bare.

There was a girl
   who searched for mercy;
She found none anywhere.

There was a pig
   who snouted for human spite.
He got so fat on it, he died of it.

1950

1951

Thou, who grew so pure
   on this earth,
that Jesus was thy flower
   at his birth;

Thou, who stood alone
   at the Cross
and wept for thy own
   and the whole world's loss;

Thou, who saw their spears make scarlet flowers
   in His side,
wounds which were His, scars that were ours
   as He died;

Now take this rose that was so white
   and is so red
stained with the blood which from Him bled.
O Mary Mother,
   it was thy own they shed.

1951

Solitude
2

Where's the poem?
   in the word, in the rhyme?
Neither the linnet, nor the lyre
   holds music's magic,
Schubert's fire.
What explains Rembrandt's line?
   not the canvas, nor the light;
Nor is woman's beauty
   in her thigh or on her breast;
And love is certainly not
   not contained in either.

So silence shall be the song
   I'll learn to sing,
when a dumb hand shall speak
   all the love I need.

1951

1954

Solitude
3

There have been many; only one,
Whose memory does not touch some bruises on my mind.
There have been many; only one,
whose image is not an accusation:
regret at the best,
remorse at the worst,
either because my kindness was cruel,
or their cruelty was unkind.
They loved being loved:
not fond of me
but of flattery;
not faithful to me,
but to their own vanity.
Your love alone was a gift, not a claim.
I learn that lesson slowly and
now let you go again
      with difficulty.

            1954

1955

Easter Lullaby

Lord Jesus once was a
    child like thee,
Yet there has been no
    other.
Lord Jesus laughed once
    just like thee,
    For Mary's delight, as
    you delight me.
Weep, child, weep for
    Jesus' Mother.

Lord Jesus once had hair
    like thee.
    His could have been no
    softer;
With skin as smooth and a
    mouth like thee,
    And eyes that had wept
    before they could
    see;
Sleep, child, sleep for Jesus'
    Mother.

    Lord Jesus once had toys
        like thee,
      Throw, child, throw your
        ball higher;
    And hands that His Mother
        kissed like me,
      Hands that my hands
        nailed to a tree;
  Weep, child, weep for thine
        own Mother.

Easter 1955

A Canticle for Briony

Whose blood is this
That bleeds upon the rose?
To whom does
        the quiet grass grow?

Whose tears are these
Now falling from the sky?
Whose grief drags out the tide?
Whose sorrow fills the sea?

Whose hope is it
Which lifts the blackbird's wing?
Whose joy is it
That makes this sweet bird sing?

The joy is His, the grief is His;
His sight looks through your eye;
The hands you use, the feet you wear
Are His as these words too.

3 August 1955

Now the East Wind
   Hunts the tired year:
Biting with ice,
   Freezing with fear.

By a thorn hedge
   The creature lies;
Even the moor mourns
   As the year dies.

Gently the snow
   Falls on a leaf,
Bending it down
   With secret white grief.

1955

To D.

No logical contradiction
between us;
but merely, a complete
lack of connection, now.

1955

1956

The Need
(Birthday poem for Rose Marie)

At twenty
   you were the distraction
I concentrated on:
At thirty
   you were the meditation
which I brooded upon;
At forty
   you are the temptation
I will not resist.
   Time makes its creases
But your loveliness increases.
Youth is but a bone which years dress
With something more durable than flesh.
Wear your summers proudly,
Flaunt your winters too.
Put your age on gaily like a scarf.
Forty Aprils lie behind your eyes;
In them I see all May's squandered treasury;
In them I'll look in your autumn, for my autumn.
My eyes are blind unless it's yours they see.
You doubt me? True, you are too old for flattery,
Too young for vanity. What then can I give you
As an appropriate present? Diamonds are too cheap,

Furs tawdry; money would profane.
No, I will give you something
   which others want yet only you may wear:
It cost me nothing, it's all I have: my need.
So wear that weed as a rose,
   Run down the garden of your years
With it as an emblem emblazoned where I rest.

August 1956

Solitude
4

Why do You
   laugh up Your sleeve of night
   watching me, lonely, without You,
   knowing You did not give me the sight to see You,
   nor the strength to seek You?

What perverse pleasure do You find
   playing cat and mouse and hiding from the blind
   teasing the already torn and tormented mind?

And tell me: why did You have to give my eyes
   which can only stare at her
   and do not even glance at Thee?
   Why did You lame me so
   That I can run – to her
And cannot come – to Thee?

Cannot Your divine and imprudent purpose be fulfilled
Unless I deny Thee so that You in Your turn can then, forgive me?
Is my weakness indispensable to Your strength?
Are we tied together – a tin can to a dog's tail?
It must be or You would not have made me so
   That I can kneel to her
   And will not bend to Thee;
   That I can reach for her,
   And cannot rise to Thee.

1956

Solitude
5

If I were a Prince,
These memories of you
Would be all the jewels I'd wear;
   That instant I saw you,
   No second set harder
   No diamond cut sharper;
   That first time you took me, –
   What royal ruby burns
   Red as your lips were?
   My opals and emeralds,
   The sight of you sleeping;
   Your tears are my necklace,
   Those pearls at our parting.
Since I am a Prince in you
These are the jewels I wear.

1956

Solitude
6
Poem on a Painting

To the lake of my aloneness
   No river flows
I am contained by mountains of my making.
Without wave I wait, wanting; but no heron comes
   and no swan goes.
The Day delivers its indifferent glances;
Night passes merely pausing to adjust
   an artificial rose.

I hold nothing but reflections;
I wake to my own shallows, I sleep soundly
   without repose.
Will no appled boy paddle in me?
Or sunlaced girl dive and swim in me?
Has no one a boat to float on me?
Must I to quench my throat, drink myself up
   and drown?

1956

Solitude
7

Murderers are merciful compared to me
   who with the same intention
     lacked their resolution
And failed, but not from kindness, I was never without cruelty,
That you know; nor was it that I had no need, that I know;
For my peace, I had to put you to rest,
                        And so I tried
Several slow ways to kill you,
                    yet you have not died.

You will remember my first attempt
   which lacked a dagger's courage
     or a poison's quick relief:
How I struck blindly where you were most vulnerable,
At your love, and where I knew you were undefended, because
   you loved.
I did not use a knife; my words were sharper
                 As I denied
My love and watched my words wound and saw you bleed
                      yet you have not died.

And at that failure, how I next sought
   to strangle what I'd weakened
     though it had not died, though I then sent you from me
And told her, and her and him that you meant nothing to me

Knowing they from friendship would tell you ...
                    Christ! how I lied
And tried to hide the wound you were that blossomed in my side
                    yet you have not died.

But out of perversity you have grown stronger
   as though you fed upon neglect
   and were nourished by starvation;
And so, at last, I brought you back again to see if familiarity
      would kill
What had only flourished when we parted. And how I next
Belittled what you gave me, and urged myself to continence
                    till you complied
And let me be as faithful to her as you remained to me,
                    yet you have not died.

Even though I then drove you to another
   Hoping jealousy might do for me
   What it had failed to do for you;
And how I then used to come and sit upon the bed where you
      had lain –
                    or should I say had lied?
Yet savoured your betrayal
                    pretending we were identified,
Managing to absolve myself of responsibility to you,
                    yet you have not died.

But have become the mongrel at my side
   I run from only to seek;
   As a blind man, his guide,
So on you I relied; not for my existence, but for my being.
Of what use were my eyes unless they saw you? My hands
Unless they touched? ... That dependence
                    I abhorred, defied
And deliberately tried to hide from that unwanted bitch that
      dogged my side:
                    yet you have not died.

But lived a restful life within my restless sleep
   So that all my dreams were webs
   To catch you on the wing,
Or like busy streams pretending to turn from you

Only to flow to you. Peace was where you were, and you were
    in my sleep
As I'm in yours ... Thus do we two lie apart, but not alone,
    certainly not divided
                         As night's tide
Turns and makes us wake to loneliness:
                      Yet you have not died.

Though I have sought within this wilderness of thought
    To murder what I loved,
    Knowing that was suicide,
For we are what we love; but not mercy, self-survival
Now makes me keep you and your memory alive in me,
    And now I have lain you in this verse
Live there after your life in me
                when I have died
For, till then, there is no way
for you to die in me – though I have tried,
                though you have tried.

                                            1956

1957

Solitude
8

Do me a favour, treat me with contempt;
   Laugh at my poetry, say my last play's dull, a bore,
Not half as good as one I wrote before.
   Find where my faith hides and what my ideals are –
or were, then ridicule them. Beg for my heart
   And when I give it you
   Bounce it casually on the floor, –
                    No more!
That's not enough! Do more!

Make lonely my own home: rid me of sleep,
   And if and when I do, play patience with my dreams,
Shuffle dexterously, mark the whole pack;
   And when I wake, see that it's not from you.
Cheat me of purpose; deprive me of my wit,
   Make me despise myself
Assure all my friends' derision –
                    No more!
That's not enough! Do more!

Cuckold me with a painter – anyone will do
   For me, or you! Inform me of the day, the hour, the place
Make sure I hear the details – tell her
   In secret, leave the salt to her: omit no item

Or dimension; do as all bitches do –
    exaggerate one or two
        brag it was better than before
                      No more!
That's not enough! Try more!

Find where I'm vulnerable, then stretch the wound,
    Borrow my money – there's an idea for you!
Try breaking my pocket since my pride won't bust
    Then when I need the cash, say you gave it him!
You'd think that ruse would work, but if it fails:
    Promise to dine with me; come late
                  No more!
That's not enough! Much more!

Make me complain, then say you'll give him up,
    Swear vows or try at least to produce a tear or two
Till I, to stop the flow, beg you to forgive
    Me – for making you do what you did to me.
Now comes your chance; reconciled and grateful
    I drop all my defence
    Aim straight, wound where I am still raw
                  No more!
That's not enough! Do more!

Betray me utterly. For that you'll need
    Some new device; a mere fuck or two won't do.
Even when you admit that lapse was not
    From weakness but deliberately done:
That your vow was false as the groans you faked for him. No
    any cunt
    Can do that trick. Try something more:
                  Much more!
It's not enough! Do more!

What could it be? Where is a poet hurt?
    Ponder a while – what's made 'em bleed like hell before?
When digs into their pride and pocket failed?
    What drove da Falla mad, made Minton drink,
Pushed poor Van Gogh till he removed an ear –
    Or was it something else

Or more? You'd know if it were that!
                    Think more!
That's not enough! Think more!

Think what it was bust Schubert's mighty heart.
   That's it. You're getting close! You're getting warm, I see!
Yes; we all share the same sincerity.
   So hunt out some token which I gave to you
Sell it. Tell what I told you through my eyes
   In secret. Play it down.
Not just the moment, cheapen me
                    No more!
   You've tried all that! Get more!

Get dentures loose, then henna up your hair.
   Deflate your breasts, achieve a spotted thigh, be smug,
Be slovenly in your dress, shifty in your eye
   Acquire indifference. Oh, for pity's sake,
Do these things which time will do to you –
   For all the rest you've done
   Yet I still love, as I have loved before
                    It's not enough?
Find more! Find more!

                                        1957

1958

Solitude
9

Damn and blast you!
You behave like a pickpocket,
   or an absent-minded thief,
Raiding my sleep, when you don't even need my peace;
Stealing my heart, when you certainly don't want my love.

And all this done so bloody gracefully,
Done out of perversity, done out of sheer caprice,
Till I am undone, utterly besotted.

True, it's not your fault, you're not to blame:
Your sleight of hand's so practised, you don't even know you do
    it
And can't even think who it is
   who now complains bitterly –
    because of his anonymity.

I tell you beauty like yours should be punishable.
What right have your eyes to run up and down the street,
    creating this disturbance?
Your breasts are urchins; your lips, ragamuffins;
Everything about you is delinquent,
The whole of you gangs up
   to chuck pebbles through my fragile maturity.

But one day, madam, I'll read the Riot Act to your thighs,
And claim back all my property, bit by bit, till I am whole again.
Till then, do not reform,
Treat me as an unguarded barrow loaded high with grapes, or an
    unstaffed stocking store,
Snaffle my peace of mind, knock off my capacity to work,
As for my reputation, I value nothing which you do not take;
Nor want these rags, the remnants which you leave.

1958

Instead Of Mobile Worker
Song for Britten

I'm a psychic patient
Devoted to Saint Freud.
My trouble is: I have none;
I'm kitch but not schizoid.

My friends have perversities
I've nothing but an itch;
Where they get understanding
I merely sit and scratch.

At sessions in Harley Street
I'm morose with despair
Seeking a neurosis
I fail to find one there.

My dreams reveal that I am
Disappointingly quite hetro
Indeed I'm so bloody straight
I'm nearly going mental.

My childhood was quite happy;
My wife and I complete;
Odd whatever I desire,
She's queer enough to greet.

I'm a sort of misfit,
I simply cannot cope,
Sanity's my burden
I haven't got a hope.

                     Searching for Faith and Love.

                                   1958

Snapshot

Autumn like a pheasant's tail
   lifts over the hedge.

An old man sits in a deckchair
A paperbacked novel on his knees
                   not reading;

His worried wife forks
feebly round her border of michaelmas daisies;
                   not hoping.

Along the lane, a small girl with a pink bow
Runs home looking as contained as an apple;
                   not knowing.

A labourer pushes his bicycle up the hill
Passing beneath the copper pavilion of beech;
                   not seeing.

A poet walks through the village
And like a pickpocket possesses each
                   not belonging.

                                   1958

Solitude
10

Just as I used
   to wear your old sweater
Preferring the rag that was yours
   because it was yours
to anything that was mine.

So now I wrap myself
   within this loneliness
Preferring this fact and its cause
   because it is yours
to any dream that was mine.

                                         1958

1959

Epitaphs For Ronald Duncan

1

He was a man of such considerable promise
   in so many directions
he achieved absolutely nothing
   in any one.

1959

2

Searching for his anima
   he became a slave;
Looking for his God
   he reached this grave.

1959

Solitude
11

Leaf that I am
   unfurling from branch that is you
   leaning upon this evening that is you
Fish that I am
   swimming in the lake you are
Or as a bird
   borne by wings which are you
   up into the sky of you.

                                        1959

Solitude
12

You have planted so many trees
   In the wilderness I was
That I now lose my way
   In the forest that you are.
You have flowed to me
   With such tenderness
I now drink from the river
   Which you are.
You have moved so much into
             the ruin of me
So many toys, so many songs
I am entirely furnished by you
I have become your home.

                                        1959

Solitude
13

Lightly as willow
   leans over a river;
Gently as petals
   fall onto a lawn, she lies
with one knee over my thigh, her head
tucked into my neck, sleeping soundly
So soon after. Who is she?
Her name is Virginia
But that is not who she is: She is woman
              Anonymous in sleep,
              Immortal in this now.

                              1959

Solitude
14

Dearest, it is no longer true
   For me to say I love you
Or that I desire you though that was true
   A day or two ago, before you took me to yourself
   And from an individuality
   Made one identity
   To which we each are part and now belong.

For me to say I love,
Or that I still desire you
   Would be as tautological
   as tactful,
   For we are in that state
In which there is no predicate or object,
   Those who are separate
                love at lower rate.

                              1959

Solitude
15

Her moss of sleep upon the bark of night,
Her surf of dreams upon the tide of rest;
So do we lie;
The lark of now into the song of sky;
Our leaf of love upon the tree of time;
   The wind blows, my blind hand knows
Sight, touching her breast.

1959

Solitude
16

Now that we love
     watch how the world conspires
To wreck, ruin and upset
     this raft of our desires;
Now that we love
     observe how Time will cheat
Us of that coinage
     we do not counterfeit;
Yet now that we love
     restrain all tears, just laugh;
Let joy be our purpose
     a smile, our epitaph.

1959

Solitude
17

Dearest, since I cannot say why I love you
Let me tell you how I love you;
   I love you as a tiger loves its prey,
     intently, fiercely;
   I love you as the ivy loves its wall,
     closely, tenaciously;
   I love you as the lizard loves the sun
     completely, sleepily;
Dearest, if I must live without you,
It will not be life without you.
   Those who are born only once, die only once;
   That is not our fate. But I am content in:
   the mercy of your being.

                                                1959

Solitude
18

   As wet lilac bruised with scent
   Leans on the air indolent
   And allows the wind to break
   And permits the sun to slake
   Its fierce thirst and quietus make

   So you, my love, allow
   And give, and add to it your vows
   But do not seek a pledge from me.
   Your vows give me my liberty,
   Your eyes describe my tyranny.

                                                1959

Epilogue

In the forest of my dreams
    My fierce desire
Tigers her movements.

By the river that is sleep
    My slow eyes
Serpent her breasts of light.

Like a gorsebush that's on fire
    My quick blood
Stallions her loins of night.

Across the desert of the day
    My blind hands
Weep for your presence.

1959

The Thought

Why do you run away and kneel
behind your eyes?
Why must we rake our lips
for broken words,
when we could know each other, openly,
and find the core of our desire,
rich, as the poppy's fire, though it fades ...
Now, why must we tear at love
like this?
And why, must I bleed – before
your kiss?

1959

Solitude
19

You think this makes us equal: nothing will;
You say there's no difference: in your doing this,
Because I'm doing that. Let me tell
You there is a difference: I am that difference.
   The proud stallion of my will was not made
To pull this cart of damned equality;
I was not born to argue or persuade,
These are my hooves! That for humility!
   Now mount me, give me free rein, hold on tight,
And arrogant we'll gallop over these equal lawns of night.

1959

Solitude
20

   Because I have looked into your eyes
I count myself the best read man in Europe.

1959

Solitude
21

Loneliness is our thirst,
Other people's loneliness:
     the only water to quench it.

1959

Solitude
22

I have at last come to terms
   with your curtains;
I can now look at them for what they are;
They no longer hurt me because you made them.

And slowly I am making my peace
   with your garden.
I see your bulbs now like fingers through the weeds;
They make me sad, but it is a sadness I am learning to accept.

It is your pile of flat stones
   by the gate;
Those you dragged bravely up from the bed of the stream
To make a path with,
   it is that which is so belligerent
   and will have me on the run.

                                        1959

Solitude
23

Does the wind move the branches
   or the flaying leaves cause the wind?
It does not matter – the wind blows.
Three trees stand there on the bank – two ash, a scrub oak
   between them.

As the gale funnels up the valley
   the two ash trees shew pliant, their branches combed by the
      wind:

But the oak stands rigid: then suddenly its great trunk breaks
    asunder.
Which tree is the stronger, the ash that bends
    or the unmovable oak now too splintered for timber?

                                        1959

Solitude
24

Dearest, do me a favour
    Treat me without mercy;
Let your cruelty
    Run free, so long as it runs over me
Love me as the wind loves
Waste me as water is wasted;
Ask and demand all from me, take the whole of me;
For only when you take that
    Can you give me, me.

                                        1959

Solitude
25

Madam, if you are unaware
    Of the effect you have on others,
Then you must be insensitive, blind and wholly irresponsible;
    But if you do know,
Then that means
    you are cruel, immoral and unkind
As your kind.

                                        1959

1960

Solitude
26

Most people are unhappy
    because they can't get what they need; shew them
No pity.
   They at least know what it is
They want.
   They have their desire: if you were to gratify it,
You'd only deprive them of their purpose.
    If you have any loose pity to spare, throw it to me –
Who doesn't know what he wants,
    though he feels the lack of it.
Whose life is spent running frantically
    without a destination,
Generally proceeding on one course
    then in precisely the opposite direction
Always arriving late, where he did not wish to be;
    Always hurrying from where he should remain.
Oh chuck some pity in this rich man's hat
    Who's beggared of singleness
Who's expensive clothes hide a threadbare soul,
    worn to a draughty laugh,
Patched beyond piety,
    with his bare doubt sticking through the arse of his vision
like a baboon; no like an overfed pelican
    who's thrown so many titbits of affection

He doesn't know what to eat
    and expires in plenty from starvation.
    Who, with too much understanding,
is unable to make a choice;
    with too much tolerance for anger,
Too much knowledge for belief
    and not enough for faith,
Too much caution for action,
    not enough for decision....
Oh leave a tip for this white-tied guy
    who sits at this table dining alone
Fearing that she may come,
    yet hoping that she will not.
Oh pity the divided heart
    ours is another poverty.

                                        May 1960

Solitude
27

The Philanderer's Lament

It's all very disappointing: most disappointing.
   This lets me down badly – no, that's not the way to put it,
Not the way at all, not at all.
At 30, I had higher – I mean lower – hopes than this.
In those frantic days, this poor unenthusiastic philanderer
Had to perform – le mot juste – a sort of shuttle service
   between Bayswater, Kensington and Hammersmith,
     with an occasional peremptory invitation from Grosvenor
        Square
All very exhausting, very –
    especially having to remember
Which women had given me which tie
    and those links I was wearing...
I think I can claim that in one Winter
    I drove 15,000 miles through the jungle

Which stretches from Oxford Circus to Notting Hill Gate.
And in those days, whenever I could snatch a lonely night
    – pretending to have the 'flu, hoping to develop mumps,
I used to lie awake and look forward to my 40's
    with something that passed for resignation
But was secretly smug complacently.
    For I'd been told that these fires died down,
That I would become less of a dog tied to that tail ...
    Apparently I was misinformed.
For here I am around the 50's,
    Still standing at the foot of the Nelson Column,
Still, at the beck and call of every unwitting female.
It's all very disappointing, most disappointing – and
    unfair too.
After all, this is supposed to be an age of Equality,
    Yet so many of my friends have respite
Denied to me.
There's Possum, safely passed his prime – not that he notices it;
And George Devine: my God, I wish I were impotent as he!
It's disappointing, most disappointing.

                                        May 1960

Solitude
28
For V.

    What can I do with my love?
      I can make my eyes
        a window for you
          to see through.
      I can make my heart
        a home for you
          to live in.
    My lips shall speak to you;
    My ears listen for you.
      My manhood will be the poppy you pluck.

From my need, I will weave a basket
   where you belong.
I will become to you: and be kind
   as your own skin to you
That's what I'll do with your love.

September 1960

Solitude
29

Any man might miss
   Your lips or thighs, but I
Miss the slut, the shrew in you;
And hate this quiet peace which lacks your nasty tongue,
Bored with my bed too big without your bum.

Any man might want
   You for your charm, but I
Want the bitch, the nag of you;
And walk this slow evening so dull without your spite,
Sick of my thought, less you're distracting it.

Any man might love
   You for some part, but I
Love you whole, even your heart,
In which I am contained, though I've not entered it,
– Or so you say sometimes, only because you wish to give it me
   again.

1960

Solitude
30

All right, run off with you and go
But let me warn you, Madam, where you go, I am.
   The more you run from me,
   The more you run to me,
What you become, I am.

You seek another lover? Oh don't deny, or lie;
That's a useless thing to do to him
Who's made all these frailties his own.

But let me ask you: what quality has any other man
   Except he is not me, –
A somewhat negative attribute, you agree?

All he could be at his poor best
Would be to be deputy, understudy,
Plagiarising my hands, aping my eyes, parodying my lips,
And it's you who'll cast him as this stand in
To watch him try what I alone perform.

But I'm not jealous, give him encouragement, it's all you'll yield.
And all he'll take from you will be your tolerance,
Your patience and a yawn.

And don't think I'm being arrogant
I don't despise him. You misunderstand me there:
It is that I, being so sympathetic to his role
Am, he, at one remove.

And don't apologize; I have reached that point, philosophically,
   Where I perceive all lovers only labour and perform for me;
Extended thus, spiritually,
Insulated so, emotionally, I achieve
   Both the ease you denied me
And the anonymity that is yours.

1960

Solitude
31

Dearest, be ruthless:
   give me more love
Or give me more disdain
Abandon your pose of pity,
Stop teasing me, show me contempt;
Love of our intensity
   should be violent to be tender:
It's your kindness that is unkind.

Dearest, be generous
   give me more love
Or give me more despair
Either yourself or your emnity:
Stop liking me, be cruel and hate;
Love of our intensity
   should be savage to be gentle;
It's your kindness that is unkind.

1960

Solitude
32

Words are a net;
Feeling, the water escapes through the meshes
I fish for silence.

1960

Post Card For V

Last night, my knees searched for you;
    my thighs wept for you;
and like blind puppies, my hands
    whimpered for your breasts.
This morning, this child
    folds his napkin, shaves a greying beard.

                                                        1960

Solitude 33

Thou, on a Cross; I, on a divided heart.
No other point of identification, but the nails;
Mine of indecision. Forgive me, for I do know what I do:
Do to her whom I love, but not exclusively;
Do to her whom I love, but not completely,
Two hands, two eyes, two legs and two feet:
Choice is not possible, amputation's probable.
Only my love is whole: each is a part of you.

                                                        1960

Solitude 34

Because my eyes have stared
So often at you
People looking at me
Should see your image impaled upon my face.

                                                        1960

Wind Song

I am as hungry as the wind
and would
I could
around her bare body
bind, wind, twine myself
till her
clear skin glowed so
that she would only dare:
dress her smoothness,
salve her freshness with
my live gentleness, wind – my wantonness.

1960

She, Who's My Music

She, who's my music, says:
  'Lack of your song from
  surfeiting, tell me? Or
  has our sun certain summer of strong love
  lessened essence, silenced spring's adagio,
                    done for
  your violin string gut quickening,
  fret and thrill of your
             asking for
  me? Ah! me.'
Thus, she who's my music, says:
  'Will you sing?'

1960

Solitude
35

I spoke to my sadness and I said:
Why d'you lie upon me like this, relentless?
With all the clumsiness of a dumb ox's dull tread
Tethered to a fixed point of penitence

                                                           1960

         Easter:

         Two days after
         We hung him with
                 our jeers,
         nailed him to laughter.
         To-day he rises:
             Resurrected in our
                      tears.

                                                        1960

If you persist in concentrating
   on obtaining sexual satisfaction
You will grasp nothing
   but the awareness of your desperation
   leading only to further desperation.
It is not that you have anything to learn
   You have everything to unlearn.
This flower can be plucked,
   by those who do not reach for it;
This rose is held
   by those who do not grasp it. You have now let go,
Even as I for another reason let you go
And when you do you will hold it, as I hold you.

                                                        1960

The München-Gladbach Lyric

Today, I am sad,
    sad as stone things are
In their stillness;
    or as old toys are
In their loneliness;
    as a room is
That is empty;
    as a child is,
That is lost.

This sadness clothes me
    as sparrow's feathers
fit a sparrow's wings;
    closely it lies over me
completely like a panther's skin
    over the panther,
giving its savage stealth
    the quiet sheen of night.
So do I walk, wearing your absence
    like a crimson robe:
Proud of my grief, Prince of our parting.

Let others be beggared in gaiety,
    I will sit here rich in my waiting,
Quiet in my wanting.
    Clothed in this sadness I wear
What you have woven;
    my silence speaks:
All time shall hear
    what this dumb heart has spoken.

1960

Solitude
36

Lobes of mauve lilac
Lie indolent on the evening air;
Waxed white magnolia, children's hands in prayer;
And over the wall aubretia sprawls
For bees to paddle in its waterfall;
And all about my grazing eyes
A green world in innocence lies.
Grateful for my solitude I keep
Company with my thoughts, and fall asleep.

1960

Solitude
37

Mountains are merciless as man
    Their cruel teeth savage
    Throat, flank of sky
    Tearing into song of vein of thigh
    Wounding flesh of light of night
    till the tortured rivers ran with blood

        Or

    Like dugs on an upturned sow
    They give suck to mouthless clouds
    breeding the barren
        out of their granite breasts
Mountains are for man, not for me.

1960

Solitude
38

As thrush, lark and linnet are
   So do my eyes rise,
Sing for the life in you
   Joyful at your being. Oh
          be there

Where I am going, when I return to
   Be bark to my ivy
Tree to my climbing
   Be merciful
          be here

Where my hope is, be there where my home was,
   Else I am lost, lonely as driftwood;
Be to the restless river, me
   Clear pool of no purpose
          be still

Peaceful as grass is, grow gently,
   Secretly beneath
Impetuous rain of me
   Be brave at my cruelty
          believe

In my gentleness; forgive me for this,
   Forgive me for that. Contain my disparities;
Accept my extremities. Oh love me wholly, so
   Holy shall you
          become.

1960

1961

Solitude
39

You ask me to write a poem
Not because you like poetry
But because you like me,
And want to give something to me.

But because you are humble
(Modesty is another thing)
You do not offer me yourself, but myself
Knowing that is what I have lost or absentmindedly mislaid,
And that is something I shall not find again
In her, or her or you.
But might in moments like this to which you lead me
When I sit fishing in silence from a shoal of quicksilver words
Which leap like salmon the instant that I look.
It does not matter where I look
   at petals of lilac falling to the grateful lawn;
   at the tractor trailer burdened with its load of dung;
   at her, or her or even you . . . it does not matter,
Anything which lives is poetry.

The restless swallows dive for flies, hunger is their song;
Watching them, I am, I find that self whenever I do not belong.
So now I can give you this,
                    the self you give to me.

1961

Solitude
40

There was no part of you
  my hands did not know.
Now separated,
  let the memory of my hands
Enfold your neck, your breasts, your thighs,
  gentle as petals fall
  or the wings of butterflies rise.

Be like a chrysalis contained by my fingers, encased by my
    touch:
Let the rude world stare at this robe you wear
  Dior could not copy it
  Paquin imitate it;
Go dressed in my hands, my desire the designer
  Clothed in this passion
  You are the height of fashion.

So flaunt the memory of my hands proudly
Till this blind glove with which I now write
Can undress you, and from your nakedness
Receive its flesh, its purpose and its sight,
Embroidering your skin in the fierce tattoo of night.

                                                              1961

Solitude
41

Now that our love by life has been betrayed
And the whole fabric that we wove is rent
By bitterness, by hate, and argument,
And all our hopes by disappointment laid
And nothing's left but lawyers to be paid
And what we owed each other is misspent

Till we have nothing left but our resentment,
As my wounds were the only thing we made.
Now that friends gloat, usurpers snatch the bone,

While friendly neighbours gossip viciously
And we are each homesick without a home
Because your smile was the one home to me

   Let me say I will not mourn though our love dies,
   Let it! I don't care! For see, here it flies!

                                    1961

The Gift

Since she whom I love
has a gift for jealousy;
I – a talent for adultery,
We reached that point where
We kept our friends in conversation;
Lawyers in fees, and ourselves
In something that passed for anger,
But was more like grief.

Now I see I must learn to love
her jealousy:
it being a part of her,
And hope that she can love me
for my adultery.
But this she's done. This she's done.
Could it be her jealousy was a gift,
A gift to me?
We have begun. It is not done.

                                    1961

Postcard

When all this place is rubble, ash and dross
As it will be, and no-one misses the loss,
When my untidy life has reached its tidy end
And you sit old and cold with memory as a friend,
When the years have worn you,
And worry torn you,
Then read these lines and feel my love again,
Remembering we rode the high places of this world together.

1961

The Mistress

She possesses me completely;
I am at her mercy: she has no mercy.
One moment, she lies quiet as milk
the next, she flings the night or my work in my face.
Sometimes, she encourages me and flatters me,
at others, she scratches till I bleed with remorse,
Her moods are mercurial.
She is all extremes, entirely inconsistent.
I live alone, only to discover
Loneliness is just another woman.

1961

Solitude
42

How fragile this frightened sparrow is
   which I clasp in my hand;
If I clutch it, to keep it,
   I will crush its wings;
But if I release my hold
   it will fly away.

So fly away, fly away!
   Let my love be your little wings:
I cannot, will not, hold you
   knowing that where you go, I am.

I will be the air that bears you up,
I will be the branch you rest upon,
Your flight from me, shall be to me:
   where you go, I am.

Oh fly away, my love, fly away!
Look! my hand is open, only my eyes are closed . . .
Adieu, my love, adieu.

What miracle is this? Its fear has gone!
Now it makes its nest within my fingers.
It is a cage no more, it is her home.

                                        1961

Solitude
43

If our ability to love
Can only be assessed by our capability to forgive, then my
  darling,
I must be grateful to you for teaching me the language,
Though I confess I've sometimes found it difficult
To articulate all the charity you earned
And was till now often dumb with resentment, bankrupt in my
  love.

The fault was yours; how could I learn to forgive
If you failed to confess? I blame you there,
Your modesty and reticence made me backward
And my Elementary Love remained in the Remove,
Not knowing the tenses of maturity
Or the conjugations of your sex.

How could my love develop, if it
Had so little to forgive, and I was always the one
To be forgiven? No wonder I remained
Still learning the alphabet
While you graduated from tolerance to indifference.

It was not kind of you to keep me illiterate for so long.
Knowing your virtue, taught me nothing but that I lacked it.
True, I admired you for yours; but since I thought you faithful
  to me,
Your virtue was something I left for others to forgive.

If I've been jealous it was because
I thought you were giving them lessons you denied to me.
That this was not the case, and they had nothing to forgive
Does not alter the fact that I now sit here for my examination
Without having had adequate preparation.

Your little perjuries were not enough
To teach me charity. Neither were your fits of envy
– I mean those of me – sufficient for my education;
Nor was your frigidity a fault to teach me
Anything but pity; and pity has no more to do with love
Than desire has with compassion.

You were of course quite generous to me
In your long deception: I thank you for that.
For if you had told me frankly at the time
That you had been unfaithful to me
I would have had nothing to forgive –
Except that more temptation had come to your door
Than I had often found in my gutter.

No, it was not your long deception
That is my present lesson. That's too easily understood,
Too easily forgiven. It's one thing to tell a priest –
But a husband tends to be more attentive
And less impartial as a confessor.

Besides which, as I know we sometimes
Hide the truth from those we love, not for our own protection,
But for theirs. That you did this to me,
Was no more than to quote me to my face;
And though I tend to resent my own faults seen in others
– plagiarism flatters as the devil only knows.

And of course women have their own temerity,
They can't brag of their adulteries with effrontery,
They have to be secret in order to be kind; as Sweeny says:
Somebody has to pay the rent; and as that's not them
What else can they do but go on nourishing their indiscretion?
Though the worm gnaws at their breast, they can always wear a
  bra.

No, your lies and adulteries give me as little to forgive
As your insensitivity did – or does.
And, of course, I know you would have been more honest
If I had been more understanding. To condemn a woman for her
  lies

Is as unreasonable as blaming a bird for its wings.
The best we could do would be to resent the fact that their flight
Is always more sustained than ours.

Similarly, I realize that you would have been more faithful
If faith had been more fashionable. And was I not
A leader of fashion – we'll not refer to taste?
For there to be forgiveness, there must be anger first;
And the more I hear, the more sympathy obtrudes.
Now what can I learn of love, if I've only fashion to forgive?

Even if you'd used your pretence of virtue
To double my sense of guilt, so that I had then become
Untrue to myself, as I had been untrue to you,
And if that had then made me abandon her
And lose my self-respect – even that I could easily forgive.

For when a woman helps a man to lose all self-esteem
She does him a greater favour than she knows
Or maybe she intends. Yes, even if you had done this to me
And made me lose a woman's love, that would have been a favour,
Certainly, nothing I could not forgive.

You claim that's what you did? Then it seems you are forgiven –
Poets, my darling, are born with love. I did not need your lesson.

1961

Solitude
44

How can we be parted
Since we are no longer separate?
The train that conspires to take me from you
Will only take me to you:

You will be on the platform to greet me,
You will be in the taxi beside me.
Though I may speak to others
I shall be looking for you.
When I walk I shall be walking towards you,
When I sleep I shall be lying beside you.
Because we are no longer separate
We cannot be parted. Yet I dread the world.
That does not hold your eyes.

                                        1961

1962

Clasp For A Mislaid Necklace

Here's the ground she and I, let our
love lie down on.
Look at it, just like any other bit of turf,
but nettled, now. –
To keep it private, so others can't love there?
Or is it earth's game merely to shew
That if we'd loved well – something should grow, or be born,
there?

1962

The Horse
(written for the Horse of the Year Show)

Where in this wide world can
man find nobility without pride,
friendship without envy or beauty

without vanity? Here, where
grace is laced with muscle, and
strength by gentleness confined.

He serves without servility; he has
fought without enmity. There is
nothing so powerful, nothing less
violent, there is nothing so quick,
nothing more patient.

England's past has been borne on
his back. All our history is his
industry; we are his heirs, he
our inheritance.

1962

1964

Poem Written At The Request Of A Political Group

Excuse me, forgive me if I interrupt.
  But I want to ask a question.
  That is what poetry is:
  Not a description, not an answer, but a question.
  And the question I want to ask is:
    Who are they?

You are all and always yattering about they.
  You say: 'they have made it!'
      'they might explode it!'
      'they are irresponsible!'
      'they must be made to realize!'
        But who are they?

Forgive me if I interrupt, but I would like to state:
  that each man is his own fear;
  that each man is his own armament;
  I mean: You are they.

The thing which we have to fear
  is not the thing, but our fear;
  for it is our fear that has made this thing.

Forgive me if I merely sound offensive,
   when what I wish to do is to insult you to your face,
   And tell you that I can see the fear in your heart,
   and am therefore not surprised to observe
   the bomb in your handbag.

Forgive me for letting you down,
   when you've every right to expect that a poem should do no
      more than pommard a rose,
   But I suggest that so long as each of you worship refuge, you
      deserve to be destroyed by your own atoms;
   that so long as you would hoick each other's dentures out,
   To defend your own hearth or husband,
   You deserve that moment when it will rain behind your eyes,
   when your hands will lie like severed gloves on the floor.

Excuse me for interrupting; certainly, you may sit
                      down Madam.
I agree: let's forget what I have said or that I
                      have spoken.

                                            1964

Lines For N.S.'s First Birthday

You stand upon the lip of an abyss
Which mankind took a million years to cross.
Yet within twelve months you will leap
Across this same glacier of time
And from your sweet dumb stare you'll reach
easily to the easy miracle of speech.
Then Prince of Words, Emperor of a phrase
        you'll share that throne
Where Donne and Dante sit. As their heir
their language shall be yours
And all poetry, your own.

                                            1964

Solitude
45

How leaf we are;
   At first, all furled in separateness:
Peeping out with little vanities and hopes, also vanity;
Perhaps the last vanity, holding us to that green world
Our life shall be; believing ourselves
   So individual, we all reach, being identical.
Shall the prodigal gardener weep?

How leaf we are;
   At last, all seared in brittleness
Curled up with tiny fears and hurts, also fears;
Perhaps the last fear, tethering us to that dry twig
Our life's become; then knowing that we are
   Enumerable, we fall, being expendable, all.
The gardener is blind. He will not sweep.

How leaf we are
   Like waves we do become; first urged, then merged.
That gardener is a fisherman;
That fisherman's asleep.

                                                             1964

1965

Carol

Where the earth floor was puddled with
   urine; damp straw
In the manger; draughts under the door.
But it was appropriate that He
   should be born there
               who was to live in me.

Then the crowds bored and listless,
   a few stop to jeer,
The rest move off to watch a juggler,
But it was appropriate that He
   should be born there
               who tried to speak to me.

Where the rough nails were driven
   with malice, his hands
clutch a poppy and the petals drip.
But it was just that He
   Should bleed so,
               who had to bleed for me.

And those two women weeping
   who washed his feet with tears,

> Tears for Him and for each other.
> But it was as well they
>   should cry so
>   who had to weep for me.

1965

Lullaby
(for Virginia's son)

What falls more lightly
Than lilac to a lawn?
   Those eyelids over your tired eyes.

Who grows more gently
Than grass, moss or lichen?
   Your tiny limbs reaching through the loam of night.

What sleeps more softly
Than mole, mouse or kitten?
   Your fragile dreams weaving their unbroken thread.

Who wakes more gaily
Than thrush, lark or linnet?
   I, for the boy of you;
   I, for the joy of you.

1965

The Geography Of Women

At 18 they are as Asia:
  quite impenetrable in certain parts.
At 25, they are as Africa:
  many minerals revealed, still more unmined.
At 35, they are like the United States:
  good organizers and sound technicians.
At 40, they are as Europe is
  lusting for their past, whoring with the future.
At 55, they are Australia to all:
  a continent of which one hears a great deal but never visits!

                                                      1965

They tell you you're a pretty girl
I see what they mean. But the surface
Is not enough for me. I do not see you but through you:
At the ugliness that we are;
At the lust that we are, the fears
And all that loneliness too;
It is because I see you as you are
That you are grateful to me:
None of us wish to be invisible.

As to your being a woman.
I should know. But it is not as simple as that.
Be grateful to the masculinity in you.

And I suppose everybody hopes you'll be happy etc.
But I don't. Contentment and comfort
Will put you asleep again:
I like you alive and awake;
I give you this gift of as much suffering as you can bear:
Which is all there is to being.

                                                      1965

To The Bishop Of Coventry

I wish to ask you a question;
Though I do not expect you to answer
   not because my question is irrelevant,
   nor because you do not know the answer,
but because you do.

You tell me that God became man
   in the person of Jesus.
Do you mean wholly or partially?
If he was a man, did he know a man's
   burdens and temptations
As I do, as you did?
   Did Jesus have testicles?
Did he masturbate at fourteen,
   fornicate at seventeen
And serve a man's servitude to women?
Surely he was man in entirety,
   so do not deny him his wholeness
or holiness.

Only from temptation can tolerance derive;
Only from passion, His compassion.
So do not castrate Jesus;
   that is an unkind thing to do;
Do not divide Jesus from Christ;
   Do not make Him impotent,
for pities sake.
   It is not that God became Man,
   but this man clawed his way up
   where neither of us reach
or know.

1965

The Mill Leat

Here, where the modest water flows
   over smoothed pebbles
      past the rose,

Where stones and roots their secret keep
   and trees stand sentinel
      then fall asleep;

Where spring and summer tread the ground
   with leaves and weeds
      In their brief round;

Let us stand by this leat to know:
   We are of water
      where it flows, there we go.

                              1965

For A Dying Woman

She lies propped up by pillows,
Her pink hands clutch the sheet like a bird's feet in the snow.
Her eighty years heavy in her eyes,
Shawled loosely round her shoulders.
They say she is frail. I do not see frailty.
What rock is there strataed in darkness
Diamond with strength of will?
Or where is there a river flowing
So that its tide can ebb and flow at its own volition?

Compared to her a gale is listless
And every star is impotent, for every star is dumb.
Life does not lie in mobility,
But only in consciousness.
I do not send her flowers, but this
her own life that is in her,
the articulated point in a blind and dumb universe.

1965

Written On A Girl's Table-Napkin At Wiesbaden

If he were to walk into this cafe
I doubt if you'd notice him
Nor know how long he sat there alone
Stirring his coffee, perhaps smoking one cigarette after another

As though waiting for somebody
But without an appointment,
Nor would you notice that he was gone.
If he walked beside you, you would quicken your step.
And if he spoke to you with his slow eyes
You would look away and order another cocktail.

You would mistake his gentleness for effeminacy.
You would call his kindness, weakness.
You would have no time for him.
So why not take off that crucifix round your neck
And hang a corkscrew there?

1965

Solitude
46

Love is in the loving
   Not in the receiving;
All in the giving,
   yielding to the unyielding.

The horizon recedes:
   Knowledge is in the unknowing.
The secret is in the seeker;
   The journey is the destination;
The mind is all of creation;
   Prayer is the only God.

                                          1965

Solitude
47

Handkerchiefs are the vultures
Feeding on the bones of goodbyes.

                                          1965

Solitude
48

In my time, I was here too,
But you did not notice me sitting there alone,
Stirring my coffee, smoking interminably
As though waiting for somebody
   But without an appointment

In my time, I knew you too
But you didn't listen then
To what I had to say,
Nor could you find the time
To read what I had written.
I remember I once offered you my love;
In return you gave me a cigarette.

In my time I endured your indifference.
Now I am beyond it: you must keep it to yourself.

1965

For WSC[†]

Our grief is not for his death
But for our own life which his loss diminishes;
While he lived, he lent us a courage
We did not possess; a resolution,
To which we were not inclined;
And by some alchemy made us who were blind
Perceive a vision bright within his mind.

[†] Winston Churchill, ed.

The weary feet, the broken hands, the wounds were ours,
The fortitude was his. Like a sculptor,
He determined the height that each of us should be;
Making small men tall, weak men strong;
He carved our history and signed this century with his name.

Whatever faults or virtues men have
This man had them in extremity: being whole in being
Where we exist merely in a part. Sensing this, we, who are many
Mourn for him who, from his own uniqueness,
Made us into that few.
We grieve for a man we did not meet,
But knew.

1965

1966

For Margery and Don

Just as the same square-winged buzzard suddenly hunts
Over the bracken cliffs, forever
Hovering, forever pouncing on its same prey, rising and falling yet
Never vanishing completely, in spite of Time's deceit and

Death's counterfeit; so too, this child renews.
Under another brow, the same undying eyes look out again.
              This proves
Nothing perishes unless it's born again. From death this
Child returns, to birth our dead sons go,
And only the unessential part of them is lost.
Nothing that's precious is beyond your means –
           When only love's the cost.

                1966

Lullaby

Sleep, my baby,
   sleep as quickly
as water in a river:
              Your Mother's arms about you
              To catch you if you fall.

Sleep my baby
   sleep as lightly
as lilac on an evening:
              Your Mother's arms about you
              To catch you if you fall.

Sleep, my baby,
   sleep as gently
as raindrops on a primrose:
              Your Mother's arms about you
              To catch you if you fall.

Sleep, my baby,
   sleep completely
as scarlet in a poppy:
              Your Mother's arms about you
              To catch you if you fall.

Sleep, my baby,
   Wake as joyful
as linnets lift to heaven:
              Your Mother's arms about you
              To catch you if you fall.

1966

1967

The Survivors

Whose boots are these
   Piled high beside this oven door?
Whose teeth are these which grin
   Without a lip to frame them?
And all these heads
   Which dignify this straw,
and severed hands which lie like crabs
   upon this scrubbed tiled floor, whose justice put them there?
Who framed what law?
And what's in these sealed metal cannisters
   kept deep within the earth? How many
Many unborn eyes do they intend to blind?
   And why this store of cardboard coffins? Is there no end, no
     end?
   It seems there are two miracles: one, man;
The other: that he survives his humanity.

                                      1967

Solitude
49

I had hoped that
just as coarse grasses and withered weeds
Slowly move in, and in time, completely cover
a mine tip or a bombed site,
So would habit, work and worry
eventually camouflage the slagheap of my heart;
And to this end I let any distraction grow:
labouring to forget you.
Then casually, if not unkindly,
you visited this wilderness:
And all was ash again.
Now I have not the strength for any further
Perverse husbandry, and live
knowing this waste is me.

1967

Solitude
50

My unhappiness had become a second skin to me:
Enclosing me completely;
Something I took for granted: woke to
And lay down in: the part of me I cherished,
Because you were its cause.
And believing you were happy
I was able to carry my own unhappiness:
thinking it was a sacrifice to some purpose,
a condition of your contentment,
Or, at least, a small contribution.

But now that you tell me
That you, too, are unhappy
I cannot bear the weight of my own any more.
Even so, send all yours to me:
if he has your laughter,
And I your tears,
in time, all of you will come back to me.

           1967

Solitude
51

And he reached that point
When leaves alone listened
And the soil only seemed to understand,
When only the light embraced,
And the night cherished;
When the linnet lay with maggots in its wing.
Now let the thin wind laugh
over his indecipherable epitaph.

           1967

Solitude
52

If you had died
    then death
would have given me
That certainty which is death's certainty;
That mercy which is death's mercy.
But as it is my life's become

that death you have not died.
I see nothing, looking for you.
I hear nothing, listening to you.
And when I speak, it is because
I think you are by my side.

                                    1967

Solitude
53

It rains behind my eyes.
A gale blows through my mind.
The great waves breaking on the beach
Are feeble compared to this tide within me.
Neither women nor work
Can quieten this energy which rages within me.
Only music, only Schubert,
Can contain me; for the rest, it is waste:
That word: my epitaph.

                                    1967

Epithalmium

Since nothing of itself can be,
Or seem to be, either philosophically,
Or empirically, and even darkness
Depends upon the light; and Sirius is blind
Unless our eyes give it sight; just as the rose
Requires the evening, and the evening waits upon the rose,
So do we each exist individually,

Imprisoned in our personality,
Until we love. Love is our only window:
It is the glass through which our sad souls see
Briefly. Know this to know, especially to-day,
The gift you give is all you can receive.
So hold back no part, yield recklessly,
To find security
In being. Each hurl yourself away to double one another.
Through this window is our hope, our becoming.

1967

For Sir Francis Chichester's Return

There have been many boats, many sailors before you
Who with a sunburned hand held a creaking tiller,
Their rigging stiff with salt, their sails slack from the wind's
    indifference,
Alone, staring at the sea's confident expression of infinite cruelty.
And the world's imagined corners have all been turned before:
Even your skill is not unique.
Or rare, to this cobbled quay which saw the Golden Hind tie up
And Raleigh, then Bradford, sail away.

Why then have so many of us
Who know nothing of the fascination of little boats,
And even hate the sea for its submerged brutality,
Found ourselves following each leg of your voyage,
Sharing vicariously your discomfort from our easy chair?

Perhaps the answer is, though you sailed alone,
Each and every man knew he was, if not with you,
At least in your predicament?
                            The whole of humanity
Was your invisible crew. For now man knows,
For the first time, knows:

He is alone.
Though we have wired up our wilderness, the wind howls
    through the wires;
We are alone: space yawns at our dilemma.

Your courage is the cargo which we need
For our voyage in which the journey is the only destination.
You've sailed for us, Sir, who dare not move at all.
So, to this City which denies you its Freedom,
Receive all poets' welcome.

1967

1968

Solitude 54

I am nothing, if not honest.
And in all honesty, I am nothing.

8 February 1968

Solitude 55

Our urchin love was brief;
   A homeless vagabond, a thief,
which broke into my empty heart:
   The swag; this heavy grief.

1968

Solitude 56

Come to me, Death,
As I came from birth;
But with more speed:
Aware of my loss,
Grant me your gift I need.

1968

The Lake

The tranquillity I find by this lake,
   Does not come from it;
it derives from my mind.

Walking the surf swept beach
where the sand is untrodden
And waves, with hands of surf,
   reach for the pebbled shore,
it is not the sea
   which lends me brief serenity;
   This peace I find
is jettisoned from a tide within my mind.

Nature's measurement is cruelty,
               which is not unkind;
The sea's a torture chamber,
               without punishment;
Rivers writhe knowing no pain;
               roots twist, feeling no agony;
The whole Earth is a grave,
               but only I can grieve;
The sky is empty, there is indifference,
               no sadness there;
The universe is void, until my mind's sorrow
               fills it.

1968

Solitude
57

I ride, the road winds uphill;
A thin wind blows;
It is raining; it is night.

I ride, the road winds uphill;
A thin wind blows
through my mind;
It rains behind my eyes.
It is night.

I ride a dead horse; the road is lost.
The wind blows through my mind;
It rains behind my eyes;
It is night.

Both the dead horse I ride and the road is lost.
My mind blows;
My eyes rain;
It is night.

My weeping eyes are blown before the wind;
A riderless horse
treads them into the road.
It is night: the night is me.

1968

Solitude
58

Why is it when we ride together,
My horse gets winded
              while yours still gallops ahead?

Why when we walk together,
Can you always run back home
              while I trudge on half dead?

Why when we bathe together,
Do the waves hurl me under
              yet the spray doesn't touch your head?

And when we listen to music,
Why is it my eyes are wet,
              and from yours no tear is shed?

Why when we lie down together,
And I sleep because you are beside me,
              do I wake to a lonely bed?

Why do you still smile, when I get angry with you?
Why do I seek you, when you are by my side?
              which of us two is dead?

                                    1968

Solitude
59

        Love passes; grief does not.

                                    1968

Solitude
60

Your death took everything from me
        but my life;
I am left walking where we walked,
Sitting where we sat, riding where we rode.
At night I turn her to me
But my lips are on your lips,
Our embrace empty;
I have become your shadow;
Which of us two died?
   Both. They buried only one. This corpse walked away
A shadow without object,
A ghost searching
      for his death.

1968

I would that my love should grow
   without a heart to feed upon;

I would that my heart should feed
   without a life to lean upon;

I would that my love should shine
   without an object, without a shadow;

I would that I should die within myself
   and live in my love for you and you and you
   as He did, yielding without possessing;
All other love is death,
   is death's amorous dissembling.

1968

1969

Solitude
61

I have now become grateful for my worries,
thankful for my financial difficulties,
and pleased that I have this burden of a farm
with all the repairs of a small estate.

I am obliged to the Inspector of Taxes
who interrupts my meditations;
the telephone's ring is now as much a consolation
as the innumerable forms I have to fill in
with frivolous and irrelevant detail.

Even when I have the toothache, I am glad,
and I give thanks for the nail in my shoe, for anything
That distracts me from the wound, the hurt, the pain of you.

1969

Canticle
(for Thomas Eastwood)

1

If gratitude is a prayer
Then even I can pray.

2

Those who have walked
The dark unending corridors
Of their own despair, and have trod
That corkscrew stair where
Regret leads and remorse follows,
and who have known that distress
when the thought of suicide
came as a caress, they who have stepped back from such sadness,
they alone know gladness.

3

Now my eyes laugh for their light;
my veins sing for my blood;
My days are all delight
Since I know each hour's been stolen
from that womb where only maggots quicken.

4

Therefore I sing, grateful for the sun
which tigers the blue prairie of the sky
stalking the fallow moon which bleeds with darkness
till the udder of the light
is milked and it is night.

5

And I who have imagined I was laid
Within that damn indifference of the grave,

Must sing of fire: glad for its warmth,
Glad for its friendly flames.

6

And my moist lips must speak
That word which is the most important to them: 'water, water'.
With my throat's gratitude I repeat: 'water, water'.
May the fingers of the rain touch me;
May the hands of the river play over me.

7

If my eyes could speak they would sing
praise for the shape of each and anything,
grateful for each colour too,
especially for that gentleness
which clothes the fields with green,
the sky with blue.

8

And if my feet had tongues, they would show
gratitude for the earth they trod on,
the earth that yields us,
waits to receive us,
   Oh Earth, I am in love with thee,
   As with a woman, I am in love with thee.

9

To be is to accept life in its entirety.
I am grateful for pain
which alone can measure
the mercy that is sleep;
I am grateful for sorrow;
Is sorrow not the lawn
on which joy dances?
Yes, even for death I am glad;
For death gave me
This gratitude for life,
   Oh Life, I am in love with thee,
   As with a woman, I am in love with thee.

1969

A Syllogism
(for a Counter-Tenor)

Truth is derived from events;
Events are made from mistakes;
Mistakes are the result of ignorance,
Ignorance is derived from lies
    Therefore: truth is falsehood.

1969

In Delhi

Beside these bougainvilleas, Gandhi fell
   Grateful to his assassin
Who had performed a service
                    greater than he knew;
The Mahatma, a disappointed man.

Now beside these bougainvilleas, people
   Pray by a flower covered monument.
It is a habit of mankind to turn dangerous men
   Into innocuous religions

And so castrate them. The Untouchables
   Are still Untouched. The land
Still possessed by those who do not cultivate it.
   The Mahatma, a disappointed man.

1969

In Dublin

When I peered into the bog of Irish history
And considered the barbarous cruelty
   Inflicted by the Vikings and the Irish
                on the Irish,

And glanced at the savage idiocy
Imposed by the Normans and the Irish
                on the Irish,

And smelt the moronic bestiality
devised by the English and the Irish
                for the Irish,

It seemed remarkable to me
that there were any Irish in Ireland
left to endure
                the Irish;

Which will no doubt soon be rectified
Now that the Irish have suffered
                the final humiliation
of rule by the Irish.

                          1969

Legend From Vancouver

You ask me where we came from? I will tell you.
   Once upon a time, a million buds ago,
There was a beautiful girl who lay down to sleep
   Above the bend in that river.
She had eyes like a sloe; breasts and thighs
   smooth as a sea-washed pebble.
Every night while she dreamed, a lover came to her,
But he would never let her see him,
He would never say his name.

So one night, she rubbed the juice of walnut between her legs,
   And put ash on her breasts and soot on her hands.
The next morning, she saw these marks on the chest, thigh and back
   Of her brother.
Then she ran from him in horror.
   And he chased her up into the hills.
So she turned herself into the Sun.
   He became the Moon.
Every night he still seeks her, after she has laid down;
And because the marks of his sister's hands are still upon his back
He never shows it.

You ask me where we came from?
   The moon is our father; the sun, our mother;
We were born bastards from their embrace.
In the beginning, as our parents were up there in the sky,
   We were lonely and lost like orphans.
So the Maker of all the other stars took pity on us:
   He gave us the leaves of tobacco
To chew or to smoke to lessen our despair.
   And then, when this failed to quieten us completely,
He gave each man a sloe-eyed girl,
   Who was not a sister,
To ride through the night
   while the moon envies him.

1969

The Fraser Canyon

Where quietness has roots; silence, leaves;
   And solitude falls through the air.
Where the bones of the earth appear:
   Ribbed with ice, fleshed with fear.

And the grieving river flows
   Beneath prisms of forgotten snows,
Where man is a dream
   The forests won't remember.

1969

Envoi

The purpose of life
   is to increase awareness, sensitivity.
It follows that the meaning of life
   is to suffer, first in oneself,
Then for the other.
   The meaning of life is to suffer.

1969

Solitude 62

Love like a storm breaks,
uproots my serenity.
No limb of me can withstand
gale of your being.
On the precipice of your eyes,
I cling to habit,
Clutch at tufts of morality,
but all's lost, all blown away
By blizzard of your gentleness;
Seeking to say myself I cry:
'Oh, love, destroy me utterly.'

1969

Solitude 63

If they should ask where he found beauty
say: 'in my lips, hair, mouth and eyes,
– easily in my eyes.' Then stare at them
so as to silence them.

1969

Solitude
64

Confound your jealousy
What crime have I committed?
Whom have I
raped, murdered or robbed
That I should now deserve
This punishment of being loved?

                                              1969

1970

Spring Song

A flock of flamingoes
   Suddenly appear perched
On the branches of the Magnolia;
the pale green leaves are sheathed,
   timid beside the blossom's flamboyance.
The evening is silent as a glass of milk
And hope shuffles in again – –

1 May 1970

Lines For My Daughter On Her Wedding Day

Here is a rose
   I planted in the night;
A vision sought
   without the eyes of sight.

Now she dances;
   On her feet I tread.
While she lives, this poet,
   Not his poetry, is dead.

May love find tenderness;
  Life learn gentleness;
And weeds and men retreat
  Before this rose, he planted
In the night.

September 1970

Solitude
65

Oblivion as a writer,
Death as a man;
This is your future:
Escape it, if you can.

1970

Epitaph For Sir Mike Ansell

Rider, rein up your horse, let it graze
  On the grass growing over this untidy grave.
And listen: that is not the wind you hear,
  But the tenant's unbridled laugh
For here lies Mike Ansell
  Blown here on his overdraft.

He laughs because at death
  He alone paid no duty,
Although he was a secret millionaire
  with all his wealth within his friends
In you and you, you, his rich estate:
  And that he declared and valued at the highest rate.

1970

For Radio Caroline

Who are all these grey little men
   pompous, and anonymous
In fat black cars?
   Creating nothing but statistics
Making only regulations?
   What is this thing they serve?

Who are all these grey little men
   anonymous yet pompous,
With their eyes focussed on other people's keyholes,
   their virility in their pencils?

What is this brainless creature they tout about
   with its enormous arse
clumsily heaping calumny on each of us,
Who, by, with and from, the people
   hourly devours the individual?

How did we, who are the heirs
   of Raleigh, Wilberforce and Winston
Reach this state where he cannot build,
   She cannot go, nor I write,
without some twirp's permission?

Was it for this servitude of frivolity
   the small boats ferried,
the young men flew?
Who will subscribe to my fund to buy Britannia
   a set of dentures?

1970

Schubert

What a saboteur Time is
   to have separated us.
Legs, and both eyes, I'd sacrifice
to have had this pen
   serve your need
As you serve mine.
What songs could we have written
If your genius with mine
   had been combined
Harnessed by our single mind.
Now only silence sings them
The wind mourning for their loss.

                                    1970

They tell me it's my birthday. How old am I?
Too innocent to be 10;
Too arrogant to be 20,
Too rich to be 30;
Too poor to be 40.
Not ambitious enough to be 50,
Not wise enough to be 60
If 70, women would need me
and love me more; if 80, my family
would look more hopeful;
If 90, they would appear more frustrated
Nor can I be 100 for then I,
     as all the world will know.
So, 15 must must be the age of me
If age is measured by maturity.

                                    1970

Vancouver

If cities could speak
This city would say:
  'I gave you everything which nature could give.
  My mountains kneel down to the sea's embrace,
  Broad rivers and streams flow through my hands,
  And a whole province of fertility lies as a shawl
  Over my shoulder, so give me back
  Some of this grace I give to you.'

If cities could speak
This one might say:
  'For pity's sake, do not build me only in stone.
  Make me into another Athens where trade
  Was in the mind and traffic in the spirit.
  Build me with the bricks of ideals;
  Make me a monument to aspiration.'

If cities could speak
This city would cry out:
  'Running up and down its streets
  Like a lost child with no home to find
  Amongst all this obscene offal of commercialism,
  The neon sores of syphilization
  Which sells the shoddy to the indiscriminate;
  Where what is tawdry competes with mediocrity
  And vulgarity spawns over all.'

If cities could speak
Vancouver would plead:
  'Let me grow to my own stature,
  Build me not in stone,
  But with the stuff of poets' dreams.
  More permanent than steel,
  More durable than concrete,
  Then furnish me with minds.'

1970

Poetry

For length: a ruler; for weight, a balance;
   For human consciousness: poetry;
   it is the instrument of definition,
The marking out of distinctions, the extension of territory
   which the mind can cultivate and colonize.
The word: a swipe at the jungle,
   the articulate undergrowth;
the right word: a sharp sickle
   precisely fashioned:
      as 'scythe' conveys the sweep of the blade,
The curve of the handle; so a plate is flat,
   and its syllables are too.
Any man could imagine the way lilac
   leans on the evening, even if he'd never seen lilac
but only heard that word's gentleness.

Words can create, not merely describe.
   They extend the keyboard of consciousness.
When you cannot articulate a feeling
   precisely, the danger is that in time
You will cease to have that experience at all.
   The ox bellows: limited sensibility;
The cock crows: hardly articulate;
   Cruel fish trumpet beneath the cruel sea,
the noise of dumbness, the shriek of darkness.
Donne did more for communication than Dr Bell.
   Aristotle and Abelard explored more,
Produced more lebensraum than Dr Livingstone,
   Rhodes or Marco Polo.

Either a mental future,
   Or there is no future; all vision in our mind,
Like thumbs our eyes are blind.

Not till the word was created
   was the universe created;
Before that this vast canopy of stars
   was meaningless and dumb,
An idiot dribbling in galaxies,
   Slobbering its finger in Black holes,
Reeling clumsily about,
   its vacuity extending
The Doppler shift of yawn. Neither energy, nor mass
   has value: only the mind can mean.

Writing a poem about poetry
   Is like an eye groping to see itself;
A mirror peering out for its own reflection.
   But words are all we have,
Words are the torch poets use
to light up the caverns of your own being:
   showing your own world to you.
Like a tiny nightlight, I am content
   if I can give even a shadow on the wall
to you, or you.

                                               1970

Solitude
66

Last night I dreamt
That all my fingernails were eyes
And that I strangled blindness with my hands
till she cried from pain for mercy;
And I showed none.
For I knew that tears alone could give her back her sight.
Then, as she looked, and saw:
   it was as if the sun had vision
   for I threw away my shadows and all the rags of night
   and bathed within the pity
   for pity is her light.

                                               1970

Solitude
67

She, who in my heart
   Has for so long lain
concealed as a chrysalis,
   And never shewn the world her wings;

She, who made me swear
   Never to reveal her secret,
Will herself, when she is old,
   Wish to flaunt it as a jewel;

Then, when they question her word
   And she is made to doubt her own memory,
These lines may then unfold
   To prove she does not lie,
And let her fly again.

                                          1970

Solitude
68

Yet would that these words could give
   Peace to my frightened heart;
Oh would that I did not know:
   life makes us live
In part; after death takes
   and breaks and leaves us with
An unbroken pump a perversely beating heart.

                                          1970

1970-71

Paprika
1

Damn and blast the Middle Classes
 with their zipped mouths,
Enormous arses
 And bugger the Proletariat
Which excels at being inferior at.

Paprika
2

Lenin, having forgotten his aims,
 Redoubled his efforts to achieve them.

† *This series of poems was written during 1970 and 1971, ed.*

Paprika
3

I put my hand into my pocket,
to give a penny to a beggar:
But finding only sovereigns there,
I gave 'Good morning' – to the beggar.

Paprika
4

St Thomas Aquinas wrote
   That it was impossible for a man to love a horse
   Because it could not return affection.
The Ass must have been thinking of God.

Paprika 5

Mr Eliot informed me that he was convinced
   That there was life after death.
I congratulated him; and replied that, for my part,
   Observation of my friends had led me to doubt
Whether life existed before death.

Paprika 6

If there's a life after death
What precisely is the point of dying?

Paprika
7

Doctor's are mere moles,
Leaving small mounds of earth.

Paprika
8

When I asked Dr Hill
    why he had become a psychiatrist,
He replied that
    he had always wished to be a sex maniac
but had failed his practical.

Paprika
9

Saints go to considerable lengths
 To describe their efforts
 In overcoming their temptations of the flesh.

 They were more fortunate than I
 Who am in danger of being canonized
 From a fastidiousness
   which opportunity fails to overcome.

Paprika
10

In England, honours come
Only to confirm mediocrity.

Paprika
11

Be well advised:
Do not try to sell aphrodisiacs to eunuchs;
Spectacles to the blind;
Poetry to the Danes.

Today I set off like an impudent shrimp
To inspect the back teeth of a whale.
Not surprisingly I was swallowed.

Wearing my best suit 'not precisely the fashion,'
And carrying several volumes of my poetry
In a pigskin attaché case,

I called at three Copenhagen bookshops,
Not as a poet, of course,
But in the disguise of a publisher,
Or at least, a publisher's traveller.

The first shop was most courteous,
But they had not heard of Mr Duncan,
And regretted etcetera.

The second asked me if this author
Wrote like Mr Henry Miller?
Apparently they had quite a sale
    for 'Sexus', 'Plexus' and 'Nexarse'.

The third gave me to understand
That it was a pity I did not publish Mr Osborne.

But I emerged unscathed:
    You cannot depress a fossil.
Genius is indigestible, it is only refined
    by being passed through the arsehole of a camel.

Paprika 12

Mr Harold Wilson says
   that he stands for the common man.
How well he puts it.

Paprika 13

The U.S. Department of Justice considered
   how to punish Ezra Pound for treason.
They started to try him, ended by trying him.
They considered execution, but decided
Hospitalization would prove less embarrassing to their image
   of great Patrons of the Arts.
Finally they released the poet to the tender ministration
                           of his wife and a mistress:
No nation ever proved so savage or unmerciful.

Paprika 14

Marriage is mutual cannabilism:
In which neither joint's an epicure.

Paprika 15

A Mr William Gaskill said
   He did not like my plays,
And seemed surprised
   When I thanked him so profusely.

Paprika
16

When Pound was in clink
He sang to me like an old crow.
Liberated to a mistress in Venice
He stirred his pasta sullenly
And sat silent:
    the man behind a mink mask
Crucified by hat pins.

Paprika
17

Confound Tennessee Williams.
It was he who convinced me
That it is not even remotely possible
to love one's fellow men.

Paprika
18

'When you are dining with me,' Mr Whoreson Smells bellowed, 'You should order caviar and not those cheap sardines. I suspect you do it to annoy me.'
'No,' I replied, 'as a tribute to your talent.'

1971

Solitude
69

Neither health nor happiness
Are as precious as consciousness.
It is better to be conscious of pain or misery
Than unconscious in pleasure.

                                        1971

1972

Solitude 70

A jungle.
When love begins, love ends:
A jungle.
When love ends, love begins:
Gloves over claws, cosmetics on crocodiles.
How hideous our humanity:
A jungle.
    Pity, pity me.
Release me from being me.
Let me crawl out from this mire, this bog
    this jungle of my humanity

                              October 1972

Solitude 71

I know what it is I seek in you:
    Your eyes: something which lies only
Behind your eyes. It is not
    (though you may disbelieve me

with some empirical evidence)
   this pretty part, I hold;
   or that emptiness, I fill.
These I could find elsewhere, even in my mind.
It is your eyes, I reach for,
   their look I seek;
a gentleness, I cannot comprehend:
   both cradle and the grave to me: this I know,
do not understand.
   And what also bewilders me
Is why or how you can need me.
   What have I got
You've not? It can't be knowledge
   Or experience (any school
Or cub) better than this fool ... Could it be
   my loneliness lessens your own
My sadness alleviates your own,
   that we have both that burden
and are each lighter
            carrying one another?

                                    October 1972

Paprika

Ten Negatives

1

You say you love me and imply
   That that places me at some disadvantage.

2

You say you love me,
    As though I had done something to offend you.

3

When you say you love me
    Why does it sound like a threat?

4

You say you love me.
    Behind your eyes I see
A waitress hovering with a bill.

5

You ask if I love you.
    How is that possible
Since I haven't yet learned to love myself?

6

You ask me why I look so sad
    When we make love?
Perhaps it is because
    I realize that it is impossible.

7

You give yourself to me;
   I give myself to you.
How's that for mutual spite?
   No wonder we lie exhausted.

8

Your vagina is like a sea anemone
   Surrounded by prawns.
I wish the tide were in.

9

If only you had three breasts
   Two cunts or a tail,
I might be interested. As things are Madame,
   All I can say is I've turned these pages
Listlessly, so many times before.

10

You claim you have given yourself to me completely.
My reply is: that is not enough.

                                      1972

Rogo Ergo Sum

What am I? This name
   which I assumed? This flesh
I feed, which fails to nourish me?
   This heart which pumps
Out of perversity? Those genes, these busy enzymes,
   This digestive tract?

Where am I? Behind my shortsighted eyes?
   Within the mind, I cannot find
And finding, cannot free? Then, where do I lie?
   What cave, holt or hole
Hides my nucleus, identity?

Do I sit within my memory:
   bones of grief, rags of disappointment,
dressed in a diary? Are these irrelevancies, me?
   And in my absent-mindedness, do I seek
To shed, sloth off these scales of me?

What is this consciousness
   I write and rave about? This awareness –
I notice others haven't got? What precisely am I?   I am this
   question. The answer is that question.
This question: that is me.

1972

1973

Solitude
72

Must I, who've searched so long for her
In this crowded world, empty without her,
Reach for her now just as time reaches out for me
And shall I lose her, because time's spent or wasted me.
No! Now is our time. There is no other
Dearest, our love will put false time to shame
And from these words, damned time though Blind and deaf
               Shall see and hear your name.

                                        27 March 1973

For My Sister

Though earth lies heavy:
   clay, a vice upon your breast;
and roots of rose
   reach for your chestnut hair
you shall not lie buried here
   since my words can lift
you, to the dance of you;
you, to the grace of you.

                                        1973

Solitude
73

Now I,
   mast high,
Carry the sail of her;

While she,
   full jibbed and rigged,
breast, buttocks and thigh
   lifts from, leans on
hull, keel of me;

Wind laced,
   spray lashed,
She rides,
   tacks and is borne, bearing;

Our prow
   cleaves waves, heals time,
And time's dividing; we race to where we are
   where desire is all desiring.

1973

1974

In Memoriam
(Kathleen Barrington)

She said:
      'One of the advantages when you're about
            to die is:
      You find you have all your friends about you –
at any rate briefly'.

She said:
      'The thing that irritates me most is: when
              the primroses come round again
      I know I shall be beneath them –
          which is not exactly the best vantage point
      from which to see those little dears'.
A woman of style; she made men feel shabby;
      Death, look small.

November 1974

The Baker

As a baker, he went from house to house
   Offering to bring the living to life
   And do something for the dead.
The women came to their doors and said:
   'Thank you. Today no bread'.

                                      1974

Solitude 74

Only because you ask me, will I write:
   For words are now quite meaningless to me,
     who've wasted my entire life weaving such rags
                      as this with them;
So, do not value this or anything I wrote.
Silence alone shall speak for me
and give you the truth
                    I never could express,
but held within my heart
                    and its distress.

                                      1974

For Karina

May this rose
   sheathed in Night
lie on your pillow
   With the light

May this lily
   the Dawn gives me
Touch your lips
   As I kiss thee.

       (another verse torn off)

                   1974

Omar Cayenne

On wings of thought
  I sent my eyes
Into the pavilion of the skies,
   There they sought the source of light
   Within the entrails of the night.

Like bats about a moonlit tower
  My hands fly through the weeping rain,
Then hanging from a brittle leaf,
twitching from fear they fall from grief.

Lips of roses
   then lead me through

Caverns where velvet flowers unfurl,
Where lizards their long silence keep,
Dreaming they're not yet asleep.

1974

Forgive

Forgive
      my talent
which gave offence
to all who lacked
      my genius, my sense.

Forgive
      my being
superior to you and you;
And what was worse:
      knowing it too.

Forgive
      my charm
I never sought,
it had no value:
      or no woman would have bought.

Forgive
      my humour
which was mostly tease:
A frequent hurt
      which seldom pleased.

Forgive my love
      which was all waste,
Mostly self-love
      and proved no taste.

Forgive
> my death
so long delayed:
> > I wished to inconvenience my friends;
> > with relatives, played.

1974

The Reason

Not for her beauty: that could be replaced
  In any city, though not improved upon;
Rather more for her mind, though here many men
  could compare, at least in reason.
So that's not it; nor is her sensuality
  The cause, and here I've no complaint.
Then dare to ask what it is you love,
  And answer honestly. I love her
  for her love: reciprocity is the reason.

1974

Solitude
75

How eloquent her leaf gentle eyes are,
By comparison: Donne was dumb;
Rochester reticent; Pound tongue-tied.

These opals are more articulate than
Language; they can sing without notes;
Plead without words; caress without fingers.

And what do her eyes say?
They tell me what I cannot translate.
Before them poetry is silent.

1974

1975

Solitude 76

What lamb's as gentle?
Which daffodil more graceful?
Where's grass grow more quietly than
Or primrose as modestly?
What spider spins more sensitively
Or panther treads more carefully
   than you, than, than you
whom blind hands fashioned
and to whom evolution, crawled?

                             31 August 1975

Solitude 77

    As April perches
    On winter branches
      So she leafs
        Every twig of me;

And as May showers
its little flowers
   So her love
   gives my life to me;

May this brief summer,
Now last for ever
   Let no one dare
   Shear this child from me.

1975

Solitude
78

Because a lady asks me
   I will tell what it is I fear
Most in this world from which I'm wholly lost,
   being possessed by her.

It is not pain, poverty, nor disease;
Nor my own death,
                for that would bring
Only release from this fear
           which obsesses me:

  that she might die before I die
And since, between us two there is one heart,
  Her death would take the whole from me and leave no part.

And because she shares the same fear
   that we, who are inseparable will be parted,
and my death tread her promise into grief's wide gutter;
   And because I know:
     pity is pitiless; mercy, merciless;
   mankind, so unkind;
     and our little raft, so frail;

Reason makes me ask:
   whether we two should not dare
To run to our death deliberately,
   as we to our embrace
with only the day to grieve,
And not mourn for one another;
Our memories still wet upon our lips,
   Her hopes for me undimmed; my fears of her unfledged?

And my reason answers:
   this is a solution
to a problem which has no solution;
   and that way it would be death,
not love which dies.

So dearest, let's take each other by the hand
and hurl ourselves at him who hunts us,
accepting the oblivion we've known so often
within each other's eyes.

                                                   1975

Solitude
79

Whose cruelty is this
   which now divides
Us from each other,
   to keep apart
Those with four hands
   but this single heart?

What strategem's fulfilled
   Or system satisfied
Which holds me here,
   while she's confined
There, within this prison of my mind?

What's Physics up to
   to let us down like this,
When it can make great double stars
   revolve, and with gravitation haul
the harrows of Andromeda
   over vast fields of space?

Why does light hurry so
   unless from spite
To show she is not here? And darkness
   Why do you fall
Merely to tease you do not bring her to me?

How empty this crowded earth now is.
   How blind my sight
Which cannot find her eyes.
   They say I live; I know I died,

This is not life without her by my side,
   bride of my breathing; bride, to whose eyes I tried
To reach for, opened mine, then, to keep her look
   Closed my own and died.

                                        1975

Solitude
80

Remember me,
   when I've no place,
But as a shadow
   On your face.

Remember me
   As we once lay
A wave of love
   With limbs of spray.

Remember me,
   And do not grieve,
When I am ash,
   for the wind to weave,

Remember me,
   Now all is past,
Your memory alone
   My looking-glass.

1975

Platform Postcard

Wheels will wear
   acres in the ache of space
and me, effortlessly:
but words can, if the wheels allow,
heal, silence distance's crying concertina.

Then,
   word to remember her lips with: 'briony':
word for her eyes:
                 'mulberry,' 'lightning' or 'alleviate';
for her breast:
            'ebony.'
and word for her love: 'Lebanon.'

                                            1975

Winter

Winter, slippered with leaves
   shuffles beneath the gaunt branches
of ash, elm and sycamore;
   only the chestnut promises
with its sticky spears.

The hungry wind mongrels the evening;
   a lone yellow rose begs for pity:
Its own petals, its only alms;
   indifference is old, winter
that much older; beneath a shorn hedge
   an old ewe lies in labour, magpies
in evening dress, wait to dine on the afterbirth;
   a shawl of starlings lifts above the trees
then rain on the bare furrow,
   and night treads across the wet fields
with its lantern of darkness
   shedding saucers of sorrow.
Winter envelopes us, we drown:
   our hands reaching out
for those absent fingers of spring.

                                            1975

It is May: still days
   stretched taut across a blue morning
to a blue evening; the nettles lanky,
   lobes of white lilac lean over the wall;
   magnolia petals float on the lawn;
It is May: a frail fresh fierce firework display.

1975

The Envoi

Dear friends, be kind, abandon me,
   of friendship masking animosity:
               I've had enough.
Gentle Earth, open up to cover me,
   of farming and its poverty:
               I've reaped enough.
Sweet sleep wake me to rest,
   of anxiety and frantic dreams:
               I've spun enough.
Oh beloved, lead me from love,
   from women's tongues, and jealousy:
               I've bled enough.
Gentle Jesus, save me from Christ:
   from Christians and their morality: take me too:
               I've had enough.
Of life, whom I once sought
   within this loneliness of thought, take me to death. Of life:
               I've had enough.
Dear God, whom I deny, do your worst:
   Keep your pity; I, my contempt. Of both man and God:
               I've had enough.
From words, may sanity deliver me
   from Poetry, finally rescue me,
of its meaningless babble:
               I've scrawled enought,
                    enough.

1975

The Poet

He did not travel up the Amazon,
   climb the Andes
nor perforate the black rind of space:
But with some temerity he explored
   the dark labyrinths of his own mind,
     and from its complexity
     brought back simplicity:
discovering, the God who lies in a pail of milk;
Observing, the unseen gentleness of the typists' fingers,
     the grace of the menial,
     his manual of grace.
His conquests made you heirs to an Empire;
Though his map leads you nowhere but where you are.

                              1975

Post Script

Nothing unique can, or could, exist;
   not even God.
If any thing in the universe
   was of itself, and independent,
it would constitute a universe within a universe:
   which is philosophical nonsense.

Whatever exists now
   must be capable of being created now.
Creation itself could not be a unique condition.
   Therefore, it must be continuous:

Prairies of stars are being born from the dust;
   Life itself, ex detritus.
Nothing could have been which could not be.
   Physics has no tenses.
Time and space do not exist.
   The only reality is: flow.

1975

Solitude
81

I have come back again.
I have got back again, at last
  to you, do you
    see my foot-sore sorrow ...
How, how can you sympathize with my heart's parched sadness,
if, at the sight of you, it reflects – only your gladness?

1975

1976

Solitude 82

The corn waits for its ripeness;
  Milk, in its quietness; the sea with its sorrow;
Roses climb to their falling;
  I live with my dying.

July 1976

For Rose Marie's Birthday

    What homes the swallow, makes
      the spawning salmon
    Seek? Who lifts the linnet,
      Throws the lark high
    To splash this wilderness with
      its waterfall of song?

    Whose hand designs
      web the spider weaves?
    Who lends the panther stealth,
      springs the tiger,

frights the fallow deer?
   Who gave my grief, relief;
lessened remorse, filled my loss?

What starts light on its way,
   turns Andromeda,
plaits the comet's tail,
   grooms the sun's great mane?

How did Schubert find?
   Who focussed Rembrandt's eye,
Guided Gaudier's quick hand
   till form leapt from stone?

And where's the listener to these questions?
And why no answer except this silence
   articulate in the slow look
From her brief eyes?

10 August 1976

For Karina's Second Birthday

From where this crimson
   bleeding from that rose?
To whom does the linnet
   pour its wine of song?
Into which wild cave or cavern
   does the wide river flow?
Where this child's innocence, its home?
   How came its trust, its truth, its hope, its charm?
Deo Gratias! Deo Gratias!

22 August 1976

Instructions At My Death

Let me lie at the cliff edge
                  outside this window;
Do not box me; wrap me in rags.
Please do *not* dig deeply;
                  cover me most lightly;
Sing no hymn, say no prayer.
Clouds my wreath:
                  champagne your requiem.
Do not enclose it with concrete,
                  or nasty chippings.
No inscription beyond my name.
The dates: irrelevant.

                                    23 August 1976

Inscription For A Drawing

Thus weeps the rose
     and everything I see;
The whole world weeps:
     grief our destiny.

                                      24 August 1976

Autumn shawls the hill;
Beech, ash, sycamore and oak
still dressed with pheasants' tails
   cascade the branches.
   Beneath these trees
the wings of butterflies are heaped
slippering my feet.
The light tapestried on an old brick wall.
A dog tails it down the street.

                      Monmouth October, 1976

Lament For Ben

(to Schubert's Trio Opus 42)

Is life, this life, his life
   now lost, was that a dream,
And death, a dream too?
   Whose sleep, whose dream
   Are we who live?
This death, his death
makes all of us die too.
   His life was ours;
   His death is ours;
We grieve, for whom?
We grieve for ourselves.

May Bach and Purcell
Bend down to this bier
But let music sing
to sing their song
Their song, their song
Though poetry's dumb.

In this waste, this grief
these notes alone lend us

† *Benjamin Britten, ed.*

       yield us
       give us
       some relief
          though brief
          though brief

November 1976

Piesport

Where the lyre
    to which these rows of vines
are strings?
Who the tuner
    pruning so carefully,
ruthlessly?
What is this music
    I hear as silence
falling quietly
    over this valley
through which the Moselle flows?

1976

Solitude 83

If they should ask you
From curiosity (which is not concern)
What it was this poet loved in you,
   Turn on them proudly:
Let them read your face,
   though winter's scribbled round your mouth

And grief has combed your hair,
   Then quietly say:
      'He loved me for my loneliness;
Thus, I suppose, the more he loved
   the more loneliness he left me with
To love'
   Then shew them the door
To sit alone again:
   As silence, I will caress you;
As your unhappiness, I will undress you;
   As your death, I will desire you.
I am your scar,
   who loves you for the wound you are.

                                        1976

Solitude
84

What seashell sleeves
               wave, surf or spray
As completely
         as she receives
this tide of me?

What branch or leaf of
         birch, beech or aspen
Is sheared by the wind,
         as ruthless as she
by the gale of me?

And where's feather
         on lark or linnet's breast
as close as she
         now lies at rest
On the grace of us?

                                        1976

Summer

Does summer
           stride through the wide cornfields
combing with fingers the ripening prawns of barley?
Or does it hide
           in the tiny corals of pimpernel,
or lean beside the lanky foxglove, or sprawl
           in the hedge where honeysuckle spills
its prayer of scent?

Or is summer
           found on the untrodden sands
where white gloves of surf
           reach for the receding beach?

Perhaps it's bound in that blue pavilion
above apple-burdened branches
           and strawberries' soft jewels,
or heard by the sound of crickets
           a child with a ball,
with a lark as a waterfall?

Is summer there
           the brief season between
Spring's hope, Autumn's disappointment, and Winter's
           long despair?
No, summer is not here, nor there.
           The only season
which can weather our despair:
           is the love we give
and to give, is to forgive.

1976

For Rose Marie

September shawls the shoulder of the year,
embroidered with briony,
    rose hips and sloes;
this month is brief with mushrooms,
slow with apples, generous with pears;
while over the hills
    the clouds graze
with bracken dreams.

                                             1976

Autumn

Keats trod here:
                no poet can follow
except borrow his images,
                imitate his sensitivity
which must be sorrow.
    All I can do is to say:
his poem on this season
    proves Art can surpass Nature,
that feeling contains more logic than reason
    and that sight is blind without a poet's vision.

Not all the Octobers I have lived,
    nor all the harvests I have gathered,
bundling their whispering sheaves,
    or bagging up the combine's spill,

milking the blackcurrant bushes,
    or breasting the Bramley's immodest fruit,
have yielded to me, to you, what his poem gave, gives;
Keats trod here:
                Winter alone can follow.

                                    1976

Requiem

Oh bugger this. At this rate
I shall soon be left to my own bad company;
Death's a greedy hog snouting us up
One by one, leaving only the unborn living.
Or like a game of skittles; few left standing,
the sod so well practised. Where's Uncle Tom,
his stoop, his caution and kindness?
Gone down the same bloody drain
Which took old Ez: my post lighter now,
Communication wholly broken. And Igor too:
That's a loss only the deaf can bear;
His spruceness, his immaculate ear
Shovelled next to Diaghilev:
Champagne cellared next to cider.
And where's Cocteau's cricket of a mind,
His natty ties and spiteful witty tongue?
Utterly undone. Paris empty without him.
Even Wystan's junction of a face
ironed out, smoothed by death's caress,
such talent and all that vodka wasted.
While my sister lies
With nettles rooted through her eyes,
And my mother sits, her stocking rumpled,
Waiting in a geriatric ward
    for a train that will not come,
telling the beads of her past,

knowing she has no future, waiting;
dying as slowly as science permits.
Not forgetting Bapu: shot in the belly,
Forgiveness on his lips. Or Einstein,
Best poet of us all.

Oh bugger this for a game. Death loads the dice,
Takes all whichever way we play.
As for me, I walk this rotten plank
Blindfolded, without faith, without doubts,
Certain only of extinction: I curse, I swear,
Anger consumes me, tempered with resentment.

1976

Solitude
85

Though I deny Time reality,
   According it no meaning
Other than a figment in my mind,
   I have found these last weeks
Longer than my patience. Time, it seems
which does not exist, persists in me.
   It is born, dearest, when we are parted.
Distance makes us die to one another,
   And waiting for these days to pass, is all the life we have.

So hurry back, drag Time away from me;
   This tyrant is now my entire reality.
I praise him in minutes, worship him in hours;
   While he, like a bloody thief,
Filches my peace of mind to fill it with this.
   What is this? It is anxiety, it is
what love is: it is grief; love is:
   Suspended grief.

1976

Solitude
86

Just as an unmined ruby
   locked within a seam of rock
burns there unseen:
   a secret in a secret dream,

So, dearest, my love for you
   Hides beneath the rubble of my life;
I write this now, so that when I'm dead
   And all your beauty
Lies crumpled in your lap,
   You may wear these words,
And to the world
   proudly lift your head.

                                          1976

Solitude
87

In the morning, I am sad;
   because to wake
   is to part from you:
You inhabit my dreams.

In the evening, I am glad:
   because to sleep
   is to go back to you:
Our love is wasted: it is as though you had died;
Whereas, of course, it was merely:
   their morality was satisfied.

                                          1976

Canto
I

If pheasant's head
   cause of pheasant's tail,
Night, consequence of light;
   Feet, reason for legs;
If spiders dependent on webs;
   surf upon waves,
tide, moon, and so on
   down to molecular links;
And nothing of itself can be,
   Then that must inevitably include me,
and limits, or erases my identity.

What then does my death mean?
   Does it imply
That I, alone, am separate
   From my background?
Or that this fabric,
   this embroidery of stars,
Perishes with me?
   That, at my demise,
This whole universe is blown out
   As nursery candle used to be?
That could be, at least, theoretically.
   More probably, at my death,
I recede into my environment again:
   Snail into shell, surf back to wave,
Just as night wakes to light,
   To be cradled by evening
Over and over, so at my death,
   I to birth again?

This indisputable,
   At least, if this skin is me;

    this skin, these cells; these cells
       these proteins, enzymes,
that nuclei acid chain. Chemistry
       assures a resurrection. Just as a molecule
Christ breathed, sneaks into my lungs,
       So shall my toe become that bracelet
Of bright hair on some Helen not yet born,
an argument which an electron microscope can prove
       shewing paradoxically:
That it's our body, not our spirit, which gives us immortality
       Of a sort ... Men dance on deathless feet,
briefly; or on borrowed genes, for a time,
       which is not theirs, yours, nor mine.

So in this sense, which is no sense
       neither you nor I can die,
cease to be, if molecules are you,
       if molecules are me.
A jig: biology to confirm it,
       little to recommend it.
How am I consoled knowing
       my arse will sit within her knickers,
my bones become his height,
       my eyes, his sorrow,
my arms embrace his grief?
       No comfort there, not even vanity assuaged,
Or satisfied.

One might as well expect me
       Or you, to be gratified by the knowledge
that since all vertebrates reject foreign tissue
       grafted, yet recognize their own, so that
no dog devours his own tail from hunger,
       no woman nibbles her own brat, even from spite,
       it follows, we vertebrates are all unhappily related:
One monstrous family
       slithering up, or surely down, evolution's ladder,
Emerging from the first jawless lamprey
       which spawned our teeth
With which we now bite each other ...
       Little consolation there realizing

    the ape that was
Lives on in the monkey which I am.
    A sense of propriety and natural order
Compels me to protest
    that creation had no right to begin before me
Except perhaps as a rehearsal
    with all nature as my stand-in,
Nor can this painful, mindless process
    be justified after I've kicked the bucket,
And thereby imposing devolution
    upon the previous pattern
compared to the epitome
    reached briefly in me.

Indubitably, man is immortal
    if molecules are man,
And the perverse and persistent continuity of genes,
    all the life he wished for.
Though flesh perishes
    It alone persists,
When maggots
    intrude upon our privacy
To hold a ball upon our bone, we are not undone,
    though visibly diminished,
For as cabbages, Kings re-enter Rome,
    Maybe with some slight falling off of consciousness
but improvement in their flavour.

    But little consolation here;
except, perhaps, to an ecologist,
    or a dung-spreader. All that we are
Or thought we were, ceases to be.
    A prospect with little future to it;
A journey with no destination
    and no return ticket. Our very
identity completely illegible; our personality
    faded and forgotten, even to ourselves;
Our consciousness, little we achieved,
    folded within the slate; earthworms thread our thighs;
Our hopes at one with our disappointments.
    Even our grief is lightened.

When we are not there for it to burden,
   When we are divided from our individuality
When what we call the spirit
   is unceremoniously snuffed out.

There are those who, seeing it is our individuality
   Which we've struggled to develop
that perishes, maintain
   that the only way to achieve eternal life
is to abandon consciously that self which death will destroy
     anyway.
   The mistake was ours.
Consequently, several paperback philosophers
   advocate that man should turn away from self-awareness,
merge himself in mob consciousness,
   the grunt of the tribe, the groan of the nation.
That fallacy is theirs.

   Nature has evolved
By having mutant genes from which to select.
   On blind knees, bleeding elbows
We have crawled from bog to bog,
   the weak falling by the way,
the strong treading on their eye balls;
   kindness, that is unkind ... All men are
descended from cowards;
   from those who could run away from their enemies.
These our ancestors;
   the brave who stood, succumbed.
The most cunning, most cowardly and most cruel:
These my forebears.

We were always superior in violence.
   If there had been equality, nature would have had
nothing from which to select. Even now those dolts
   who drool about equality of opportunity
should realize it implies the right to be unequal,
   more cruel than others, as cunning, as evil
as I am ...

    All species, any tribe, society or civilization
must inevitably perish:
    For they are each only identifiable by being static
and nothing which does not change, adapt, adjust, can persist.
    Therefore, that mob-consciousness in which de Chardin
and his ilk would merge me, sink me,
    Is so much piss to me.
If that is their way out from death,
    it is not mine. All life is murder;
All death is suicide, the murder of ourselves.
    The choice is mine: and choice is life to me.

Not all these words are wasted,
    for I see now:
That if death is that condition
    caused by my individuality,
I see death, even my death, as a friend;
    For I would rather die then, cease to be,
than yield now this personality, this identity
    which defines me and separates me.
Let them grab their anonymous molecular immortality,
    while I run to my death
and clutch my pain to me.

1976

The Ward

    The West Ward holds six:
      Our average age is 83.
    As on a station. We wait for a train.
      It does not come.

          1.
    Beneath the window, Lucy sits:
    Hair uncombed, stockings slack,
      one holed below the knee;

Her pale blue eyes unfocussed.
   All day, everyday, she takes measurements
For a dress she will never make,
   for a daughter she never had;
Her delicate hands hold an invisible tape,
   checks and rechecks, the bust, the waist,
Then, once again, calls Nurse Warren
   to bring a chair so that the unborn girl
can stand upon it to straighten the hem.
   Pins in Lucy's mouth;
The Nurse feeds her forcibly.

2.

   While beside the television set
Lies Miss E.
   Walnut skin, apple-creased;
A junction, shunting-yard of a face;
   her hair pomaded,
carrying enough scent to camouflage a pole-cat.
These cosmetics to please him whom she calls:
   'her lover-boy'.
Let's hope he visits her this autumn
   for her sake, our sake.

3.

While by one door, Evelyn,
   bolt upright in her chair;
wholly oblivious to these surroundings.
   As usual, pen in one hand, magnifying glass in the other.
The Times Crossword completed by midday.
   At tea, the Vicar calls with another book
And retrieves his calf-bound volume of Macaulay's essays
   from beneath Evelyn's chair.
A man of some delicacy: he holds the book with his handkerchief
   Since it is still wet from her widdle.
All: we are incontinent, all.

4.

   Of Maud, nothing said,
Since nothing known. Even her name.
   Found at the terminus without a ticket:

Aged 86. Been here four years.
   Talks incessantly to a visitor at her bedside:
Calling him 'Al', 'Allen' or perhaps 'Aldrick'.
   impossible to tell, the syllables repeated,
never completed.
Only he could tell us. Were he to come.

5.

By the other window, a woman
   Aged 23 — that's how she sees herself.
That's how I remember her:
   her hair in earphone ringlets, taking me by the paw.
Now she sits, month after month
   too bored to read, memories all muddled.
She asks: 'When am I going home?'
   A question. No reply.

6.

Last night, they moved Miss E's bed nearer the door.
   A sure sign. Gone this morning.
She'll have been trundled to the Chapel of Rest:
   A jam jar of flowers by her head.
Her 'lover-boy' has called at last.
   Requiescamus.

                                          1976

Unrhymed Sonnets

1

Justice? What's justice? Did Jesus or Pilate
know? Does any bewigged arse on the Bench
dispense it, or she, blindfolded, balance
those weights with equipoise?
                       While the fulcrum
slithers up and down the scale: a sitar
player's improvisation is always noise,
not music. How could any man judge a man
unless he himself was that man, and knew all
his motives, suffered his appetites, his pain
and what passes for human purpose? Justice
there ain't and never will be. Mercy is all,

and pity the one court to which I would appeal.
The law can say what is right, what is wrong;
But a fart's a fart; not every sound, a song.

1976

2

They say I am a shit because I commit
adultery from love and, what is more,
purposively, not casually
as on a whore with cash register eyes.
These prigs with their prim accusations
lie to themselves, deny their own lusts,
merely because they indulge in day dreams,
masturbate in their minds, they fornicate
at one remove. And never fuck, at least
not that anyone, including themselves,
would know it. And so their excesses
pass as probity, socially acceptable,
And, by their standards, Jack can bugger Jill
and Jill bed Tom behind her spectacles.

1976

3

Acceleration is absolute; speed
Relative. So Newton thought, left Einstein
To make the obvious deductions; Physic's
Logic is unchangeable; in spite of
Particles' apparent quirks; quarks, charms,
Neutrons, and all the rest which reside
within the Quantum Theory, they kneel,
To laws which we do not yet recognize.
It's only in humanity that chaos
is King; and nothing is predictable,
Save the individual's ability
To justify his own behaviour, blame
Others wholly; himself not at all.
This is Man's Law: it is immutable.

1976

4

Just as the Spring in tiny primroses speaks,
articulate in minute violets
with an alphabet of flowers
to make the season's language, and April sing,
So she, in little actions, shews her love,
Running for that, fetching this, seeking
for some way to serve, to shew affection;
And always she gallops up the staircase
Like a pony, then sits, quiet as milk
Beside my bed, anxious but not angry;
Concerned, but never questions; always
willing to requite, not to request. Her love unfolds
and with these small errands
she does summer me while winter wolves my throat.

1976

5

Death be more proud. Don't stand outside her door
Timid as a beggar, your feet shod in leaves,
Newspapers stuffed in your pants, odd socks
worn as gloves, your whole appearance furtive.
Knock boldly, she will open willingly,
Having sat there waiting for you to call,
Saving from her penury a small tip
To welcome you with as a gratuity.
Do not hold back, nor walk away again.
Remember it is more generous to receive
than to give. So knock and take her now
Gladly. Give her the pleasure to be giver.
Leave sadness to us who'll watch you take her.
Death be more proud, knock loud, she knows you're there.

1976

1977

Unrhymed Sonnets

6

My unkind heart, take pity on my heart
which Life has broken and love torn apart.
Why can't that tolerance which I can shew
to others, nudge some mercy from myself
To myself? Why must I stand in the dock,
A prisoner sentenced by myself on the Bench
With no circumstance to mitigate
the crime? Why does my understanding
Not stand under what I am, was, or have become?
If I can't love myself a little
Why should I expect others to tolerate me
At all? And, if I'm so fastidious
So that affection for myself is impossible,
Doesn't my sense of the absurd come to my aid?

January 1977

7

Marriage is nothing more than loneliness
Without solitude; an intimacy
Without privacy or affection,
A sentence without a crime, punishment
with no remission. It is that state
in which two people know where each is raw
and vulnerable and each can hate, wound what they are,

Scar that they were. It is a tedium,
Knowing the other's stories, taste and cruelties;
forgetting, remembering, labouring
to forgive. It is a war without an ultimatum,
waged with attrition, a siege without relief,
An armistice without a peace. It is the refuge
which we seek, when we're in flight from ourselves.

January 1977

8

What's a woman but a funnel
With three holes; two for digestion
One for gestation? No aperture for
conversation, reason or wit? Their cunts
So similar in the dark, no man can know
If he commits adultery or not.
Giving himself the benefit of the doubt
As a reward for ploughing the known.
At their best, they've only two breasts;
Giving no 'promise of pneumatic bliss, not.'
In spite of Possum's distant observation.
As sister, nags; as wives, a burden;
Only as mothers, friends; Men believe
what they say; a gentleman, never.

January 1977

9

Who is there who has not sometime, somewhere
Not thought, or failed to think enough, to end
his own life somehow and not wait for death
who'll come most certainly, in his own time
Rather then ours, unmercifully? Coming late
when we're incontinent, indifferent
Bored with being, yet far too weak to die

Decisively? Who's not secreted pills,
Cleaned the barrel, failed to find the cartridge,
Or the courage? Stalked to the cliff, measured
the fall, recoiling from the bounce. Or walked
out to sea, at least, imaginatively?
All suicide is murder, but of whom?
Of those we hope, in vain, who'll grieve for us?
Ourselves?
And, seeing us fallen, will then assess the pain?

> January 1977

10

My unhappiness now crystallizes
Precipitates, takes a precise contour,
Shape which any spectrometer
could analyse, compute, then identify.
First, it would find the wave length of self-pity
(Which is by no means the same thing as pity
for the self), next it would measure out
those elements which are compounded
Into a synthesis of hope and fear;
Hope that my days are coming to an end;
Fear, that the end recedes with my strength
Leaving a boundless void of loneliness
Misery of infinite pull
and blackhole gripping the heels of light to itself.

> January 1977

11

Iago should have been a woman as
Satan undoubtedly was; how else could he
Or rather she, know how to tempt, then blame
Men for their weakness, if they were not
the measure of all weakness in themselves?
No man can dive to such depth within
his nature as woman, who with her teeth
As a grapple, can dredge several from her shallows
And spew such filth from her pretty mouth
that serpents puke and cobras hide their heads
In shame being so similar to the female.
At least in them, venom within their bite,
And what is worse about this gentle sex
Is that they skin each other, feigning an embrace.

January 1977

12

The ash and anguish of other's grief
Has often raked my eyes while I have watched
the pall-bearers lift their awkward load
Setting it down with relief on to the ropes;
And I have wept
tears that were theirs for a friend, not mine.
There is something more painful than other's grief, the lack of it;
The widow listening to a quizz game
while her husband still lies
with a sheet over his face; or the mother I knew
who wondered whether to wear elbow length gloves,
pleased that black suited her, thinking of fashion
Not the reason for her daughter's suicide.
So it is with us, even our sorrow is shallow
Like a puddle, piss from a mare and just as soon dried.

January 1977

13

Unless I can forgive I shall corrode;
Bitterness will undo me utterly.
Blind me, punish me where I would punish others
But how? The precept is not a method.
Look at this word. Surely it must mean
'give' before? Before what? Before you commit
the offence that they've committed? Is forgiveness
Then self-knowledge? The awareness that you
could do to them what they have done to you?
Is not forgiveness then, the giving of oneself?
to oneself? Are we not all neighbours
with only one hypocrisy separating us?
Is not our true vice a sense of virtue?
The only virtue, the knowledge of our sin?

January 1977

14

My health is going; my time, almost gone.
Impatient death waits in the wings; already
Most of the cast I played with gone, dispersed
Death soon to have the empty stage to himself.
Already I sense my friends' indifference;
True, not much of that, there being few of them,
My relations feigning their grief, embittered
by my will which could not please them all.
Each wishing to be heir to an estate
They thought I had no right to build,
And as I sit here lonely and unloved,
Incapable of loving; I see Death
Steal up behind us. Not all the dead,
are buried. Some of us wear natty shrouds around.

January 1977

15

They talk of love as if it were a thing,
A commodity stocked at any store
Self-serviced and wrapped in cellophane,
Each man and everyman having a right,
A need for love, it they maintain should be
Available, like bad education,
Drains or any other social service.
Nobody sees that love is something rare
Not a gift, a thing, but an achievement
By those who, having ceased to love themselves
can find something to cherish in another
And from the depths of their humility dredge
Little pebbles up which glisten briefly
In the sun before indifference covers all again.

January 1977

16

I sit in an empty room, so crowded
Not another ghost could enter it, to stand
to sit, to stare. There's my sister
Smoking herself to a standstill, interrupting
her cough to tell me to change my shoes.
There's Tom Eliot, surreptiously
reading a letter I left lying on the floor.
And Ezra too, busily imitating Pound.
There's Epstein crumbling madeira cake
His slouch cap worn like a Brooklyn youngster,
And Ben's there too, more loyal now he's dead.
While you sit where you always sat,
One foot on the seat, the other shoeless
On the floor: my grief's in flower again.

January 1977

Solitude
88

By this bed, in this vase
  are crimson roses
I gathered from the lawn of night;
  with them, lilies whiter than the snow
Which grow where dreams graze,
  where kindness shows;
And behind these flowers, I bind
  green figments from my mind.
May this invisible bouquet
  stay in yours. This way
It will never fade,
  never fall away.

                              30 January 1977

Lines Written By My Mother's Bed

Come to me promptly,
   not as a friend
Late for an approintment;
Be not casual, at my end.

Come to me gently
   as sleep comes
when tiredness closes my eyes;
Be as comforting as my home was.

Come to me triumphantly
   as if I'd won a race
To your gentleness,
wanting no other place.

Come to me as you now come to her
   taking the best part of me;
Leaving me to mourn,
She from whom I was born.

Come not as you come here,
   Tardy, with this poor dear;
Take me quick into that night
Strike mercifully with the speed of light.

Come to me, death,
   as I came from birth
But with more speed;
Grant me this gift, I need.

                              February 1977

No Easter egg, my child,
    Because I forgot to get one.
But here's the song
    the primroses sing:
Words by a daffodil,
Notes by Anemone.
    Its melody is silence.

Easter 1977

Sorry, no Easter egg:
Only worthless words
    and thoughtless faults.
But here's this panther for you:
See how it hunts the stars
    over the veldt of night.

Easter 1977

Solitude
89

They say it is important to tell the truth.
I say it is better to know it,
    but not always to tell it.
Truth may be a virtue;
    a lie, a caress.
Is it better to tell the young pianist
    she'd be better employed making butter;
Or to inform the old poet
    that you like him, but not his poetry?
If one's tongue is gentle,
    it tells every woman she is beautiful.
What place has truth in tenderness?

It is kinder to tell a fib.
To lie completely,
   is to be completely kind.

                              5 April 1977

The Last Lyrics

1

Your leaving this morning
Is as if the bare fist of November
Had suddenly thrust itself
   through April's pretty glove.

Now the flowers of your eyes have gone
It is winter again:
a hard cold winter.

                            24 April 1977

2

I sit alone.
Your invisible arm
   scarves my shoulder:
Comforting me: at least in your intent.
   Those who wish to part us permanently,
   Have succeeded, temporarily.
But these lines make them fail for ever.

                            25 April 1977

3

Ovid was driven from his home;
Others, too, have fled to foreign shores;
   But I carry my exile as a scarf
Wherever I go, or stay.

Wherever I am, I feel alienated, a stranger.
   A relic from an age which has gone.

Here, the architecture offends me;
The people's manners affront me;
Their food nauseates me:
   for the rest, it is all muzak:
piddling through every aperture,
I suspect the women have radios in their vaginas;
The men, TV screens for eyes.
   Their only culture is in the spud.
Nobody will know I have been here:
Nor will I.

                              Jersey, 26 April 1977

4

If you could see my hand
   You would observe my fingers moving
as though they played scales
   on an invisible piano;
But there is no keyboard in my mind.

My fingers are counting again
   the number of days we've been apart;
The number of hours which have to pass
   before we see each other.

Your friendship is water in which I swim:
   I suffocate without it.
I am nothing in myself:
   I am the image of the love you project onto me.

                                       April 1977

Epitaph For Milne

Here's Milne: his feet cushions to his skull;
   His eyes sockets rammed with clay.
This man was a great cosmologist;
   who raked the shoals of stars
And helped to map the boundaries
   Of the boundless universe;
Not, never, using a telescope
   always the vision of his mathematical eye.
He was a genius:
Stranger, stand here, do not pray,
   But give thanks:
      that this man passed this way.

April 1977

The Shell

If I could rid myself of myself,
And be as empty as a sea-rinsed shell,
Then, possibly, He might find me on the ocean bed,
And say: 'Though this is empty, it is not dead.'
Then fill me with Himself instead.

But I am so full up with little me,
Puffed up with importance too,
That if He picked up this thing I am
He'd turn me over in his hand and say:
'This shell's so small, yet is so full,
It holds no room for Me.'

5 May 1977

The Last Lyrics

5

It is early May:
    both the lilac and the magnolia
gladden the wall together.
As yet not a single petal
    falls to the lawn as regret.

This is how you appear to me:
    all hope, all plans, all promise.
Reaching up into the air
    as brave, as brazen
    as the almond or the peach,
And with no disappointment
    yet lying on the grass about you.

May 1977

6

Both my fingers and the calendar
    tell me we have still
two whole days to go:
    they will be slow, they will be slow;

Time is a tease.
Time is all spite
    which steals even itself from us.

I sit here:
    dressed in my waiting,
Wanting my time to pass;
    For without you, it is as if I stare
into an unsilvered looking-glass.

May 1977

7

To-day an empty chair attacked me;
It was most aggressive, most belligerent.
Its four legs remained motionless,
   But while I stood before it
thinking of the care
   You had given this chair
All the tin tacks you'd used to upholster it
   flew out and spitefully, perforated my skin.
Failing to pacify its attack,
   I ran from the room
bleeding from small wounds
   no eyes could see.

                                           May 1977

Truth

Whether truth exists
          unless it is apprehended
Is dubious.
What is there to comprehend truth
But the mind?
          And what is this mind?
It is a poor thing:
          polluted by education,
Warped by prejudice, grained by convention:
          all self-justification
which is self-esteem;
          all self-esteem,
which is self-delusion.
          How could truth
Penetrate this jungle,
          thread this tangle,
Waddle through this muck, this mire?
It could not.

                The only truth which we can reach
Is the toe of apprehension.
                The body, the figure and the face
                Is beyond our vision,
Hidden from our comprehension.
    Our eyes peer out through the fog
Of self-deception, then focus on our eyes.
    Our minds are bounded by our minds:
It is a closed circuit
    designed to carry a minute voltage,
Exceeding that, the fuse is blown:
    and all is dark again.

Or is it that there is no truth
    here, there, or anywhere
But that which the blind mind imagines?
Instead of saying: we seek the truth,
    should we not admit:
                we seek the seeker?
And if, and when, we find some truth,
Is it not because we shaped it,
    then buried it there, for our mental paws to discover?
Truth is as love is:
    Not here, not there, or anywhere.

                                30 July 1977

Do not believe
                the truth;
Duplicity's a fact;
The opposite conceals
                Our purpose when we act.

Do not believe
                In love;
Unless you know its gulf.
Love's deft, a slick pickpocket;
    Who gives, like any thief.

Do not believe
>	my heart;
Until you know that hate
Is part of my embrace,
   – or love, at lower rate.

Do not believe
>	in pleasure;
Until you feel its pain;
Remember weeping is
   Joy's way to laugh again.

Do not believe
>	in life;
Unless you know that death
Is as our own shadow:
   Embalming with each breath.

Do not believe
>	in me;
For I am not a whole,
Divided with conflict;
   A lark, that is a mole!

July 1977

The Last Lyrics †

8

Because of night:
   morning's light is a caress to me.

Because of despair:
   hope's white wings alight on me.

Because of the gravel of their unkindness:
   kindness is both sapphire and diamond to me.

Because I know I am dying:
   this rose, that honeysuckle
      flowers for me.

9

This rose weeps
   with its own petals:
They lie on the floor
   of my sorrow:
As the rain which falls
   behind my eyes
Lies in a pool
   Of my sorrow.

† *These eighteen poems were written in July and August 1977, ed.*

10
(for Franz Schubert)

They asked him:
  Why all his songs were sad?
And he replied:
  'What other songs are there?'

Then he said:
  'All I have written
Has been written from my sadness'.

Life is a wound; death, our scar.
  Man is a hare
Pursued by the hound
We are.

11

Wound of earth bandaged by night,
  A river veined with moon;
Trees, cliff and hill
  step down to the sea
Where manes of waves
  are combed with spray.
Stars perforate the prairie of sky:
  from each hole
Violets
  Fall gently
To the hedge.

12

With what precipitous grace
  the eight-legged spider
Falls on its slender thread

Then stays suspended
   for a second, still;
Then hauls itself upwards again
Winding the thread
   back into its belly
From which it first emerged.
   Such intricate and precise development
Appalls me: would I could wind my past
Into my future. A pity man never evolved.

13

How snails the year
   Beneath November's spite,
The gaunt elms sheared and bent
   By the wind's callousness,
Stand griefless without a leaf to shed.
   I wait: not for the platitudes of Spring
But for little primroses of kindness
   to gladden my barren
Unkind heart.

14

Autumn pheasants the hedge;
   October gloves lie on the wet lane
As challenge to the tournament of evening.
   A skein of clouds
Scarves the horizon.
   The sky bleeds: its blood crimsons the ocean
With a wound which has no scar.
   Then dusk, the deer, timids down the hill
Kneeling to drink the light
   till shadows are reconciled and healed.

Now night's claw is all appetite:
    pity is pitiless; mercy, merciless,
And only murder is kind
    within the tigered wood.

15

Atlantic death waits
    to engulf piddle of my life
No trace of me shall be:
    conceit is all identity.

Looking over this trickle of my days
    I see triviality
Merging with illusion,
    frivolity befouling all.

With wave upon wave, I wasted
    tide of me with words.
All meaningless froth and spray:
    I was deaf: only the dumb hand
speaks: kindness is all its say.

16

Winter ferrets
    knuckles of the banks,
Bared warrens bolt frantic
    into the gorse's prickly embrace.

Hands of elm harp the sky;
    Flutes of starlings
melody the hedge; over the cliff
the square-winged buzzard's still.

With slippered leaves
   the year treads
Shuffling along, an old man down an empty corridor,
   outside the window, daffodils
Perceive no danger; the anemone, dares.

17

Now silks the yellow on the daffodil,
   the sheath emeralds;
Diamonds and amethysts jewel the leaf:
   the flower unfurls to tawdry all these jewels.

18

Rampant lion haunches, fells the evening;
   Blood emblazons the horizon;
The day dies, the beast withdraws into its lair of night.
The earth turns round indifferent to the kill.

19

The sky mooned with opals
   where Orion pearls light;
The azure panoply
   tents the vast desert outside
where nothing, not even the wind, walks by.

20

By starred, violet tranquillity;
  Rivers pooled with peace, so still.
Waterfalls pewter spliced;
  Powered oceans; deserts of solitude;
But Nature does not sing to me:
  I prefer Schubert to the noise of all.

The Parting

21

As a hand, the glove
  the pelt, the hare,
The blackbird's feathers, the blackbird's wing,
So, we two had a closeness,
  an affinity, and being parted now
Are not alone, but separated
  incomplete, unwhole:
Being not in ourselves
  because we reside within the other;

I do not know
  what it is that joins us –
Only this pain, now that you are not here.

22

Dearest, in the autumn of my years
  the brittle leaves of my heart
Fall to the lawn you are.

Dearest, in the evening of my days
   the rags of my hopes
Are all the robes you wear.

Dearest, when death comes to me
   My eyes will close
To see you are still there.

23

As a goldfish in a bowl
   I swim round and round your absence,
Time treads painfully upon my heels.
   I know that love is all in the waiting;
And waiting is to love.
   Come home, I swim only in your presence.
We belong, not where we are,
   But where the other is, come home.

24

Now palm my hands above my sleepless eyes;
Dawn buzzards the sky;
   My tired bones cry out for the loin
of her, the mercy that she is.
   May love lie to me, if it need be so;
   May truth be hid, if truth must hide
From me.
   Let me go to death as to her as my bride.
Oh let me stride out into that darkness,
   this child of light by my side.

25

    The violet stars
        Their petals fall
On lawns of space
    beyond recall

    A swarm of bees
        In fuzzy flight
cling like a beast
    On the bough of night

With buds of eyes
    the flowers show
leaves and trees
    their way to grow

With clouds as hands
    Death's fingers pass
Over the clavichord
    Of my past

Across the field
    a panther creeps
Drinks the light down:
    my world's asleep.

For Henry Williamson

He was a man
    with a handsome, wounded face,
Bruised mulberry eyes,
    a beaten spaniel's look;
Whose quick eyes saw the salmon's grace

And sure pen saw
           the sheen upon its skin:
Shone like 'new-cut pewter'
           as it sped up, up, and on and on.

13 August 1977

Pastorale
(for a Lady's bathroom)

I stepped out into the dark. The timid deer of dawn
   Edged over the hill to lap the light
From the deep lake of night.
   A shawl of shadows hung from the trees;
Wet grasses slipped my feet; three hen pheasants rose.
   A pigeon's noisy wings
Warned a young rabbit to still,
   Its ears pricked, its fur antennae
To my approach: suddenly it bolted,
   Its white tail flagging another to follow
To their burrow. In the mill leat
   A watching trout snapped a careless fly, a heron
Instantly swooped and took the fish.
   A dog fox with blood on its muzzle
Ran to a bank trailing hen's feathers.

   I saw all kind, unkind; all things alive
Cruel without malice. It was still dark
   Yet light enough for me.
Without kneeling, without words, I prayed
   To that God which does not exist.
And this my prayer: may nothing that lives,
   Be judged. May mercy alone hunt;
May pity devour man anywhere.

19 August 1977

For Karina's Third Birthday

Little girl,
         what is light?
Light is that miracle
         which shows me you?
It is the arrow of pity
   flying to the heart of mercy
To bleed as He bled.

Little girl,
         what is light?
It is the rainbow furled,
         which on your hair is curled;
Light is the love your Mother holds
   beside which all is dross, including gold
To waste as He was wasted.

                              August 1977

With clouds as hands
   Death's fingers pass
Over the clavichord
   of my past.

With buds of eyes
   the flowers show
leaves and trees
   their way to grow.

Across the fields
   a panther creeps,
drinks the light down;
   the world's asleep.

                              August 1977

Pheasants' feathers of amethyst,
   Magenta, crimson, burnt sienna and brown
Leaf the maple's branches
   With a mauve mantle,
As it stands sentinel
   to the undying Fall.

                                        9 September 1977

Two telegraph posts: no wires between them.
   Only the wind of resentment.
Her curiosity, casual: no concern;
   Trivia of conversation
Devoid of communication;
   Proximity, without approach;
Memories as accusations. Only their
   Past before them.
Two windscreen wipers which never meet.

                                        October 1977

For Harold Lockyear

She bore a son
   As any Mother;
Her child crying
   like any other.

She gave her child
   When a boy:
Wood, blunt tools
   and nails for a toy.

When a man
   He took to this trade,
But given a cross
   already made.

Now at its foot
   This Mother weeping,
To its shade
   All men blindly seeking.

Dear Jesus
   bleed for my unbelief
Strung, strung up with you
Strung like any thief.

               14 November 1977

He kneels to his God,
   while I pray to the void
the deaf, indifferent wind.
   Who is the more devout?

I seek justice,
    knowing there is no justice;
I plead for mercy,
    knowing there is no mercy;
This journey, the only destination.

November 1977

Now wolf grief throats remorse,
    blood regret stains
snowdrifts of sorrow;
    Chamois of self
Lies on the glacier
    for carrion of tomorrow

November 1977

For Rose Marie

To-day has been a sad day
    Not because Tarina has gone,
Nor because the Prince Rajendra
    Will no longer strike our eyes
With the thunder of his hooves,
    But because a part of you
I treasured has left.
    I beg you to replace it
With that part of yourself
    which cannot be bought
And never sold.

November 1977

For Pieta

The desert of your absence
   blows through the waste of my despair,
where loneliness is all,
   and all time waits
   and no time passes.
Oh where are the little petals
   Of your care, flowers of your affection?
What is love but the waiting?
What is love but these dunes,
               these sands of loss?

                       November 1977

Lyric

If His love is all possessive,
   Has it no place for me
Fingered with my doubt?

If Faith is all forgiving
   Cannot it find
Balm for my abrasive, devisive mind?

Yes, Jesus, I heard your whisper
   On that cross,
And know your faith doubled, by its loss.

                     25 December 1977

Seascape

White wings scissor the linen air;
   Gulls' feet the wet sand,
beaking up sandworms
      scallops, amputated crab.

Hands of surf seek the beach
   their gloves erasing tide's
Wrack and signature of weed.

Rampant stallions, manes combed
     back by the gale
Mount the receding flanks of waves
To spend their sperm
Within this world of spray

December 1977

Single Ticket

I am going where:
   I can afford the fare,
Fear no Customs,
   'nothing to declare'.

I am going where:
   you will not miss me,
Neither friends nor enemies,
   rise to greet me.

I am going where
   I shall hurt no more;
Rich in bones
   my flesh still poor.

I am going where:
   I shall find no rest;
Mediocrity
   to piss upon my breast.

December 1977

Solitude
90

If this manoeuvring is love:
                I do not want love;
If this jealousy of whom I'm fond is love:
                I want no part of love;
And if this envy, spite and possessiveness
                passes for love, let me be unloved.
Love is in the yielding, not in the obtaining.
If it is not that it is all ungloved claws,
   a savage combat in a chromium jungle.
I want no part of that.

                                          1977

Spring

Now sap squirts
   up birch, oak and beech;
Fingers of daffodils thrust
   through the leavened soil:
Ivory snowdrops peal their tiny bells;
   jasmine yellows the wall; primroses sit modest
where a shiny hart's tongue laughs;
   And over it all
lauds the lanky nettle
   beside the aubretia's waterfall.

Scaly salmon brave their way
   to cleanse on shallow gravel beds;
Homing swallows seek, swifts and blackbirds find;
   the stockinged pheasant,
still wearing autumn's leaves,
   makes his rusty call;

Hedgehogs wake, moles and voles
    scurry before the buzzard swoops;
the heron stands, dawn folded in its wings;
    and newts stay still
beneath the hem of Spring.

                                       1977

    Galoshered, shuffling up the street
A woollen scarf; gloves, buttoned:
    An old man taking his constitutional
Slowly, taking his time.
Not noticing that Time's pursuing him.
He stops pausing to stare unseeing into a shop,
    Then turns away displeased at his reflection.

                                       1977

Mike Ansell

Taller than his shadow: a man
  who is patient with servants,
  impatient only with his friends;
  we like him for his virtues,
  love him for his faults. A man
  who knows the difference between fortitude
  and courage; discipline
  and obedience. Who
  to a rude age brings a consistent gentleness.
  His perceptive hands sign kindness
  on flank, girth or flower.
  He, grateful for our sight; we, for his vision.
  There is a bright candle burning in his mind.
They say he is blind.

1977

The Anatomy Of Death

Death said: 'Why do you fear me?
        Am I not your only friend?
        Here is my hand.'
        And I found I was holding my own hand.

And I asked Death what he would do for me
When the tall grass leaned over my untended grave
And the clover's roots reached
Where my eyes were,
Where my bones bleached,
When my lips had slipped
And only my teeth spoke?
Death listened to my question.
The wind answered it.

Then I began to fear
As a child fears
          who is lost;
And I felt homesick, without a home;
As though I was to be sent away to school
          knowing the term was endless
Without a holiday;
Or as though I was going on a journey
          without a destination,
Without a return ticket;
Writing to friends, not knowing their names,
Having lost their addresses;
Facing an interminable calendar;
A clock without hands,
A bud without wings;
And those about me complained that I was gloomy,
They spoke to me of the rising price of coffee,
Of the falling value of money;
Of matters of vital importance.
My ears heard,
My bones were not listening.

And I saw only the frivolous was fashionable,
Only the trivial was of consequence to them;
Those who know me valued me,
As they valued yesterday's newspaper.
Those who had loved me, persecuted me:
   I was punished for being
And Death said:
   'Didn't I tell you I was your only friend?

In my embrace you'll lie:
   a consummation to be wished for,
A copulation, without the consequence of adultery;
I will be faithful to you;
You will cling close to me.
Look upon me as your mistress.
Come to me as a friend.'

And my friend as a token of friendship
   Gave my eyes, sight.
I, who had not been blind,
   saw for the first time.
I saw that every weed was a flower;
And there was no woman who was not beautiful
Nor any man who was not noble.
Death introduced me to them all:
   to my friends who had been unkind,
he gave me their kindness;
To thieves who had stolen,
He showed me their honesty.
   He taught me that ugliness doesn't exist,
that my loneliness was an opportunity,
   that my solitude was relative
to his company;
   And he gave a basket of larks
to my ears,
   and lent the clouds to me as a shawl,
the stars as my candle,
   the sky as my cap.
And he told me:
              love is what we give,
Not what we receive.
And Death showed me that in life
   Only death was important;
This way Death gave life to me,
As a friend, as a token of friendship.

So when I die
Let me lie at the cliff edge
                  outside this window,
Do not box me. Wrap me in rags.

Please do not dig deeply;
　　　　　　Cover me lightly,
　　Sing no hymn, say no prayer.
　　Clouds my wreath,
　　　　　　　　champagne your requiem.
　　Do not enclose my grave with concrete,
　　　　　　　　or nasty chippings.
　　No inscription, beyond my name.
　　The date: irrelevant.
　　I lie with my friend
　　who now gives my life to you,
　　As a token of friendship.

1977

　　　　For what jasmine of gentleness
　　　　　　can my blind eyes seek?
　　　　To what kindness of the rose
　　　　　　may my blind hands reach?
　　　　Where grazes the little lamb of love
　　　　　　my hungry heart could eat?
　　　　Where is compassion in this desert
　　　　　　which is man?
　　　　Why does this figure falter
　　　　　　behind me, carrying his lantern
　　　　of darkness
　　　　　　before his embrace of night?
　　　　Will not death be my rose,
　　　　　　jasmine my sleep?

1977

Women

Their curiosity lacks concern;
Their love: self-love;
Their conversation frivolous;
Their minds squalid;
They are carrion
    to be avoided by men
deprived of the necessities of bread and wine.

1977

A Woman Sleeping On A Train

With vines entwined
    upon the trellis of her sleep
She lies at ease
    as milk within a bowl;
Behind the shells of her translucent eyelids
Assiduous bees tease her mind
    with honeyed dreams.
Then through the eyes of her fingernails
    her hand lifts reaching for the apple of her breast,
And with blind gentleness
    it lies at rest.

1977

A Woman Of Fashion

Elegant, immaculately turned-out:
   Dior couldn't hold a candle to her;
Her mind: a shambles of rags, remnants
   and beggar's cast-offs;
Cartier on her wrist; Woolworths, her intelligence;
Ceaseless conversation, saying nothing;
   Not even pausing to refuel her spite;
Morality: what she does; immorality: others;
   A flow, uninhibited by thought.
A good Christian, of course: she thinks Compassion's
   a deodorant; forgiveness, what she deserves
But can't afford, taxation being what it is and so forth.
   Then, finally noticing my bored expression
She asks me 'what it's like to be a poet?'
   'It's being an exile in an upholstered hell,'
I reply. An automatic, humorless smile.
   'Or it's like being on the telephone
And never getting the right number.'
   Her expression repeated: a good dentist.
'But what would you like to be?'
   I stare at her beautiful neck.
'A murderer', I reply, 'one without mercy.'
   Then I turned to converse with the platitude
On my right.

                                               1977

For A Growing Girl

You ask the question;
You will not like the answer:
   Love is anxiety, it is in the waiting;
   In the giving and the forgiving,
   Not in the taking, or the forsaking.
   Love lies in sorrow, grows by the suffering.
   Love is a thief: it takes you with one hand
It leaves you with grief.

                                         1977

1978

A Friend

Why do I flee from you, since you pursue
knowing too well you will inevitably catch me
                in the end as a friend?

When you stood too patient by my Mother
whom I loved, why did I curse you when you at last found the
   grace
                       to take her with haste?

Why do you let me sleep, except to teach
me how to die? Then give me dreams with my soul undressed?
                Do you think only you should give me your rest?

What purpose does my one lung find
Evading you who alone can give
              ease to this tormenting, tormented mind?

And she, who loved me, and whose love I deserved to lose,
Was that the bill I should pay
            on this my last day?

Death, whom I have fled from, come now to me,
Embrace me, as a lover; be merciful, though merciless;
         Pity me, though pitiless.

                                          6 January 1978

For My Mother

1.

Greedy Earth, who now devours my own Mother
   gnawing her bones clean
When will even your appetite be sated?
Are we, who slowly walk away
   all just hors d'oeuvres to you?
Yet, in spite of your insatiable hunger
   and
Quick digestion, you take nothing
into you;
She, who was my mother lives;
   life cannot die in your fat belly
Since she whom I loved still stands within my mind, my mind.
Through this, and in this, she'll escape your filthy maw:
Even your greed will appear kindness that is not unkind.

                                7 January 1978

2.

Black earth whites her bones
Maggots make ringlets with her hair
Where I was weaned
   worms move in.

Eyes which were opals of pleasure
   pearls of sorrow,
Now limpet stare
Where there is nothing there.

Hands which I clung to
Hands which guided me
Strike a chord on a harp –
It has no strings.

Skin sea shell opaque
  spider web frail
Feather soft, now stretched
  Drum without sticks.

What thief gives
  That thief is grief
What is grief?
It is a void.

That word is never
Never to see her
Never to hear her
Never to take from, give to,
Never to say to-day;
  or hear tomorrow.

Grief is a word
It speaks in silence
These tears its language
Their meaning sorrow
  tomorrow and tomorrow.

January 1978

The Dog

Who is this friend I can ignore
  curse and abuse
But who always forgives to follow me?
  What man or woman
Has his loyalty, faith or affection?
  Where can we look to find
The terrier's alert response, the saluki's
  effectless swift grace or the afghan's

heraldic stance? There is no human pain
   or personal loss which the mongrel's
wet seaweed eyes does not respond to.
     Dogs are dumb.
Because love is only eloquent in eyes.

                              January 1978

Ethel Duncan (1891-1978)

If sleep is the way
   Death teaches us to die,
What is death itself
   But the way it causes us to make
the sleep walk of our life
   Into a run to those we love –
In other words: to wake?

                              January 1978

Epitaph

Here lies my Mother
   My loss, her profit.
My whole life's buried here
   Chuck earth upon it.

                              January 1978

The Felucca

The Felucca is a slender-necked bird
   which flies on water
Rivering its way from bank to bank
   between tamarisk, oleander and the ficus tree.
It nests amongst the reeds:
   eggs are turquoise;
Both male and female take turns to sit
   then float their brood upon an opal tide
which flows to amethyst.

                                  February 1978

Egypt

   A nation with only its past before it.
This sluggard Nile
   worms its way between its banks
signing with green: cotton, alfa, lime, mint,
   tamarisk and the stumpy ficus tree;
a narrow, a brief civilization
   wholly dependent on the mud.

From Negada to Narmer,
                close up
Amnenophis to Rameses,
Nefertiti to Cleopatra, Ptolemy to Farouk,
   a fetish, an obsession with immortality
amounting to madness:
                      all clutching their toys;
embalmed with emblems of their women,

Clearly sanity is the idiocy to which we conform.
In 8000 years,
   many kind, many gifted and sweating men,
but not one sane man
              ever walked by this river
– or any other.

                              February 1978

Translated From A Fourth Dynasty Sarcophagus

  The Thebans have conquered:
    Left me with nothing but the dirt
under my finger nails;
    watched them rape my own wife, daughter:
welcome to either; cattle and goats gone too.
    Nothing left but to cut my own throat
if I could find a knife:
    Death a release from this prison,
this captivity of life.

                              February 1978

The Quandary

The trouble
   From being as intelligent as I am
Is that the mistakes I have made
   Are the more serious
Because I have given so much thought to them.

The pity
   Of being as sensitive as I am
Is that the pain I cause others
   Is particularly hurtful
Because I'm aware precisely where they are vulnerable.

The misfortune
   Of being as cowardly as I am
Is that I am said to be brave
   Only because I lack the courage
To run away or to end it all.

                                             February 1978

Barnstaple

They are all either
   eating, breeding, shopping or
                        going
  nowhere in a hurry.

Few are
   looking, serving, praying
                or living:

>   obsessed with the trivia
>   of existence.
> None
>   concerned with the ultimate,
>   all bemused by the immediate:
>   Bees without honey, ants without
>   purpose.

February 1978

Solitude
91

Dearest, I have an admission to make:
   it is that I am terrified;
And it is right that I make this confession to you:
   because it is you I fear.

I fear your kindness
   because your concern for me
makes me frightened I might lose your care.

I fear your love, I am frightened of your passion,
   for I know were you to withdraw either
I could not, would not, live.

I fear your beauty
   for that must attract other men to you.

I fear your intelligence
   because that must make it easy for you to reason,
And to reason is often to find an excuse
   even though that might destroy both you and me.

Lastly I fear time
   of which I have only an overdraft,

And little credit.
    It is as if I were in a small boat
And had to walk a plank
    out to an ocean of oblivion;
Dearest, when I have to die,
    be there, so that in your eyes, I live.

March 1978

Though I do not know you personally,
I know you are a man
And that is sufficient introduction:
Since we are now both suffering
because of the same woman.
And because of that, I give you
    my sympathy as we must give
her, ours; but as you know
and I fear, even greater pain
    will inevitably follow unless
we desist from pulling this poor child to pieces.
You would not desecrate a Botticelli;
I would not split the canvas of a Goya.
But what we are now both doing to her
    is commit emotional vandalism.
If you say you love, I say I love.
    We must ask ourselves whether we love her
or ourselves.
    Oh pity, pity those who love.
Mercy, be thou merciful.

April 1978

Solitude
92

Do not believe
          I loved you
For yourself. That's an illusion:
          I loved you as myself.

Do not believe
          what I wrote,
Sometimes said:
          Only lies and spite
Entered my vain head.

Do not believe
          that I tried
To improve or guide.
          I lived, easily;
My only difficulty, I died.

                            May 1978

Rondo 'La Clemenza Di Tito'
From Mozart

I am dying:
The death of your love;
My sickness:
Your resentment, your disdain.

I cannot expect your forgiveness,
Only that you may forget;
If you could see my remorse:
Your mercy would be mine.

Now death itself does not frighten me
The only thing I fear
Is my memory of my betrayal.

This is the grief I live
Grief does not come with death.

May 1978

Solitude
93

A lost demented nomad, he misspent his life
   crossing the deserts of the heart
Seeking the oasis of love,
   travelling from one mirage to another,
Finding nothing there; his feet sore, his camel dead;
His compass unable to direct him,
   since he had lost his destination.

It certainly wasn't physical passion he sought.
   He knew only too well
That on any given moment, or any given day
   some fifty million erect phalluses
pistoned a rusty cylinder
   using ten megawatts
but still failing to satisfy that cunt
   yawning as large as the Grand Canyon.
He knew there was nothing there
   but delusion, but despair:
A waste of shame, given any other name.

Perhaps the sun had touched him?
   Dribbling and crazed, he went after
Friendship and affection; truth and trust.
   Four search parties are out looking for him.

One reports that he's been located
    hanging feet first from a date palm,
The hyenas, just, vultures merciful.

                                  May 1978

For Suzanna's First Birthday

Child, who birthed in gentle June,
Child, whose age will come too soon,
Child, whose emblem is this rose,
Holy my love these words enclose;
Child, who'll grow with grace and ease
Be not like me who failed to please:
    May your kindness be not unkind,
    And all your peace be in your mind.

                                  27 June 1978

In Memoriam

Here Igor and Ez lie beneath their eiderdown of stone;
each unusually at rest
both unnaturally at home
        beneath these cypresses' caress
with pen and baton now of bone.
        Not all the dead are buried.
        These two here prove
those interred, still live.

                                  Venice, June 1978

Death In Venice

Per Piazzale Roma; Alla Ferrovia; Per Piazza San Marco:
The bored tourists trudge their burdened way
Bearing their cameras, Durex and clutter of Murano glass,
Blandly believing culture is something to be acquired
Or photographed; thinking Botticelli is a pasta;
Fra Angelico, somewhere they should go;
That Dante and Cavalcanti are footballers;
All blind to the beauty of the unpainted shutters,
The hand-thrown tiles, the elegance of rusty iron balconies.
As usual I sit in Florians, now an old man
Gone at the seams, lungs punctured, blocked,
Mind going, seeing Ben here on his last brave journey,
Pushed in a wheel chair; not listening
To Olga Rudge's bitter babble;
Only her holding me together;
   in this city, I do not wish to leave.

Venezia, July 1978

For K's 4th Birthday

   Butterfly dreams unfurl
      upon her leaf of sleep;
   Their wings waking
      garden of her eyes.
   May the lawn of her days
      Be rolled and swept
   And nobody tread
   where Karina's innocence has trod.

22 August 1978

If those rodents who've gnawed or ignored my work
Should invade your privacy when I am dead
– for only death brings a poet to life –
to ask you what it was you loved in me,
say, honestly (for you'll have no need to lie
   now maggots are the logic of my mind),
I loved him: because of his passionate devotion
    to himself; because of his kindness and tolerance
    to himself; and lastly for his generosity
    to himself; I loved him because he was
more man than most men:
   more helpless, more hopeless,
and infinitely more vulnerable.
   Then, when they shew their bewilderment,
and doubt what you have said:
   let them see your hand
and the invisible ring you wear
   and add, he gave me this: his need.

31 August 1978

For Ben
(Dreamed At His Request)

How leaf we are:
               these autumn years
Curled, furled, shorn, torn
from branch, bough of our brief days.

How leaf we are:
               a bud of birth,
trodden, sodden to loam of death.

How meaningless we are:
               memory our one identity
Our music, noise; our poetry, piffle;

Nothing in our mind of worth
   but the kindness we need
But seldom find.

How leaf we are:
                 If you want love, put it there.

                                  September 1978

Cotehele

Stables: a National Trust shop:
Jars of ginger marmalade, pot-pourri,
Raffia work, home-made chutneys,
One or two guide-books for itinerant Arabs
Or leafless Yanks seeking severed roots:
        And all so tastefully done.

The tythe barn: serves cream teas
and impenetrable buns; sickles and scythes
decorate the whitewashed walls; an ex-groom
and a bewildered tweeny behind the rapacious till;
They've moved with the times, improved themselves:
        And all so tastefully done.

Inside the modest Manor, a guide stands
where a butler stood; he points out the Grinling Gibbons'
fireplace; another directs one to an indifferent portrait
Of Lady Anne by Reynolds; a fake Gainsborough,
On the wall; ceiling, Adams; culture, not our own:
        And all so tastefully done.

But where the family who drained this,
Who built it, and planted? Sir Charles runs a Steak Bar
in Barbados; his sister, a typist in Bude;

The whole tribe deprived, taxed and impoverished,
Robbed by highwaymen in starched collars:
>> And all so tastefully done.*

14 October 1978

Solitude 94

Music's no food, Olivia; it's a poison.
If you'd have loved, you wouldn't have listened.
Only the deaf dare; those with affections
fear its hurt, its sting, are raw, more:
Vulnerable to its pain; the way each single chord
Can wound and make the unhealed bleed again.
What machine-gun's as pitiless, as ruthless
As Beethoven's gentleness?
No hand grenade destroys as cruelly
As Schubert splinters with shrapnel of melody,
mercilessly. Only the deaf dare love.

October 1978

Solitude 95

Dearest, promise to be merciful to me now
>> By giving me the worst punishment you can.
Condemn me utterly, remind me of the many lies
>> I made to you: how I betrayed,
Played it double, cheated your trust,
>> Our truth, and justified my game

without more than a twinge of conscience;
   certainly, never finding shame.
Remind me of this, rub my nose in that,
   Spare me no detail, forget no incident
Of my deceit, the pain I caused,
   the tolerance I found, use your tongue
As a rod upon my back
   Thrash me ruthlessly.
For, dearest, only by being pitiless
   Can you pity me, by seeming unkind,
Be kind; my present sin is I forget
   I sinned against you over and over again,
Indifferent to your uncomplaining pain;
   So, be generous, be severe:
Send this prisoner to those cells below, give him life,
   Shackle him to his own rusty past.
This is the only way you can release me
   from that resentment of my mind
which, as a cancer grows,
   without self-knowledge as the only healing knife.

October 1978

Plymouth

The city darks, shadowed, lamp lit;
   The inhabitants creep
To welcome, fitful sleep:
   dreaming forgotten dreams, or
Fumbling for their brief embrace
   joyless release, or sustained disgrace.

Night workers emerge, plod the puddled street;
   Muffled, thermos flask and fags:
Their stint, their shift before them.
   Newspapers print their trivia of news;

Bobbies tread their unrewarding beat;
    Across the ironed Bay forgotten frigates sail,
And unremembered Dorniers
    laden with devastation fly.
But that is Plymouth's past;
    Now mediocrity's the flag; sad
Frivolity, the purpose. The City repeats its joke:
    Men are born; Men are born to die.
This City articulates that banality.

16 November 1978

Winter's Song

An old man widdling down his leg;
    or pawing pathetically;
finally folding his manhood
    into her impatience;
giving and taking no satisfaction.

1978

Dirge

Grief is not
        something we give the dead,
But what we feel when those whom we love and trusted
Prove false, lie to us instead.

Grief is not
        when we mourn a life
lost, but when we tread through jungles of suspicion
where cobras of deceit raise their lethal head.

    Grief is not
           shed always beside a grave,
But when the living live,
       and truth which is love,
       and love which is truth, lie dead.

1978

On Summer

Now my glad eyes butterfly and rise,
   their frail wings glance
   on sentry foxglove, on lupins' lance,
   circling the laburnum's waterfall,
   petal poised for their brief hour,
   over flagrant poppy, lilac flower;
   till perched upon the rose they see
   crimson sorrow weep eternally;
   while my unlistening ears record
   June's burdened bees, and all those casual sounds
   children and lawnmowers make in noisy rounds;
Then, in your garden, I stand to smell the year's re-birth,
and watch your gentle hoe caress the gentle earth.

1978

Solitude 96
Agnus Dei

But when we forgive
   do we not condone: risk
sharing a repetition of the sin
   we have condemned
and forgiven? If we are tolerant
   of intolerance are we not tyrants ourselves?
If we give freedom when
   freedom will be abused,
Are we not guilty of abdicating
   responsibility, doing someone harm,
pretending it is good? Pity is one thing;
   Mercy, quite another;
It seems we must be merciful to ourselves
   to prevent that hurt others give, and will give,
If they know they will be forgiven.
   The money-changers are the moneychangers:
He did not funk using the whip.

1978

Solitude 97

Dearest, be kind
          deprive me utterly,
cease torturing this tormented mind;
          Be generous, take all
From me, leave me no part
          Of this unbroken fractured heart,

Undo my soul completely:
>   Be merciful, go where I am not
Love whom I am not;
>   Dearest, pity the pitiful,
Leave me completely,
>   Be not by my side,
So let me run to death
>   as though it were my bride.

>   1978

Solitude 98

You want to know what love is?
I will tell you:
>   it is a triangle;
One side is anxiety; the second is jealousy;
The third is grief. That is what love is.

>   1978

Solitude 99

Dearest, your absence
> Tigers the gazelle of my mind:
Limbs of thought lie savaged, bleeding.

Dearest, our parting
> makes me a Black hole in a dark universe:
Gravity sucking myself into that vacuum
> where you are not.

Our separation binds me to your vacant chair;
   I know only this:
They do not love,
   who do not bleed as this.

One day, I know, predatory time
   will vulture us:
You will stride out to life; I, more confined, to death.
   But my revenge on our brief time is this:
You, and all time, shall know
   just how I loved:
By simply fathoming my bottomless distress.

                                      1978

Solitude
100

For Virginia

Where have her opal eyes flown?
Her gaiety, all that mischief gone?
Migrated from tenderness to bone to stone?
Could that kindness, warmth and softness
be hollowed out, mere sockets where maggots sport or sported?

And where those cherry lips
   her passion and compassion
All reduced to a toothsome gumless grin?
And her chestnut hair, where? Oh where?
What heavy lover now embraces her spread skeleton?

This question from my mind;
   The answer: in my mind.
She lives within my grief,
   paces up and down the streets of my remorse;
And sometimes in my sleep
   running to my dreams.

Look for her and you will find, she whom I loved
Still lives within my mind. Where? She's there, she's there.
It is death, not, she who is undone:
reduced to a skeleton.

1978

Solitude 101

The reason I have not written
    a poem to you for some time:
Is not because my affection is less,
    but because you have made metaphors
Out of menial jobs for me,
    given me alliterative embraces
and images and rhythms potent as dreams.
    Indeed, it is you who have written
the poem of these days; I read them gratefully.

1978

Solitude 102

My mind mothed by jealousy;
Suspicions serpent my thought;
Memory pollutes my days;
Imagination befouls my nights;
My dreams are whores
    corrupting one another.
As in a convex mirror:
    my future hideously distorted;

And such a gentle hand
  chucked this grenade at me.
Indeed it was her gentleness alone
  which sunk me so completely.

1978

For Harold Lockyear

The result of having
a heart as big as
His was – would be that that
Heart would break, be
utterly broken, and forsaken.
Because in this world
it is not possible but to bleed hourly for this world's unending
pain;
Not just for the pain the murderer feels for his guilt, for his
victim; not just for the so-called evil, for the weak, who
are not wicked; nor for the affectionate woman restless
in her lonely bed; nor for the homesick parson in the wrong
vicarage. The consequence of having a heart as He had a heart
would be that that heart would break over the disbeliever,
the blasphemer, the sneerer, the doubter and then,
When all this, and Reason
And Science too, was ranged
Against Him. He would then
Shoulder that cross again,
And trudge up that hill again,
To be nailed up there and crucified again.
For only when His heart was broken
Into little pieces was it, or any heart,
  made whole.

1978

The Rose

What is this rose?
   it is the kiss of night.
A red caress
   which hurts my sight.
Its petals fall
   as its fragrance flowers:
as brief as love,
   its life in ours.

What is this rose?
   it is all grace to me.
A wordless poem
   without fault or rime:
Its message clear
   in, out of time.
This rose is as a God to me:
   I worship it;
It, oblivious of me.

                                    1978

The notion held by scientists, philosophers and theologians
   That truth is an absolute, like a leek
To stand eventually revealed
   as each single leaf is shed or peeled
Is bunk.
   It may be vegetation, it is not thought.
Truth is not a reality, but a mental concept
   which must recede, as the horizon does,
As we approach it.
   As any leaf is removed

Another is revealed beneath it.
    Since our minds are limited
The only carrot we shall ever hold
    will be the knowledge of our ignorance.
Let that soup satisfy;
    with humility a condiment.

1978

Epitaph For A Friend

Who was it
    who nudged me when I sat lonely
and always put his hand in mine?
Who was it
    who sat opposite me when I was sad
With brown eyes like wet seaweed
glistening with sympathy?
Who was it
    who walked with me wherever I played?
Who waited for me however long I delayed?
No man of course but a god – spelt backwards.

1978

Franz Schubert

What love is this
        I feel for you
Far deeper than
        I ever knew

For any woman?
                    While you a man,
Dead a century
                    before I was born
And therefore one I never saw, met
Nor was helped, to quarrel with?
How can I explain
                    this love that is?
What is its name?
                    Constant through fifty years
Expressed in grief
                    Articulate in tears?
Why this strange affinity
                    between us?
How comes this rare accord?
                    Why you? Why you?
When there were, or are,
                    others similar to you?
From where this closeness
                    that binds me to you,
(though not you to me),
                    so that only three chords,
And then your daring, effortless change of key
Inevitably touches, releases your sadness from me?
Not cognition, recognition,
                    as though your suffering were mine;
Your scars my wounds.
What word is there but love
                    which makes me, who is comfortless,
Find comfort with you, in you?
                    Is it because your suffering was such
That mine is less,
                    alleviated by comparison?
Or is it that I know:
                    though we are separate,
different, you dead and I alive
                    our sorrow is the same?
And your melodies crying
                    with the pain to come to me?
A love that is sexless:
                    suffering its consummation, sorrow its child;

More enduring than passion;
                more reliable than friendship;
What is this affinity, shared identity
                    So that I who am crippled, lame,
Run, crutchless to the song of you
                  and with a bitten lip
and true humility now weep at your very name?

                                              1978

Only the deaf
              dare listen to Schubert,
Music is noise, or too meaningful to bear.

So with poetry,
              it is piffle or discomfort,
it bleeds with sorrow or with suffering
              great poetry is great pain,
Only the deaf dare hear.

                                              1978

A navvy with hobnail boots
              clobbers up the stairs
marches down the corridor
              kicks my door open
to grab me roughly by the pyjama collar
              then heaves me over his shoulder.
Who are you? I whisper
              knowing he is death.

                                              1978

Sleep
      blackbirds and bears
Twigs of dreams, nests in my bare mind
           with leaves of regrets, rags of fears.

Sleep's
      hand surfs to reach
Over the untrodden sands, erasing footprints
           from the deserted beach.

Sleep
      violins my failing breath
Rehearsing those chords:
           the melody of death.

1978

1979

What is sex?
It is not when he posts his cock
   into a well-lubricated letter-box;
Not in the groin, or the groan,
When he uses her as a urinal,
And she misusing him as a dream.
It is not in the tawdry tokens or trinkets
Nor in the betrayal of forgotten vows.
What is sex?
It is not in that hideous and awkward undressing,
That fumbling in pubic sores.

Love is in its gentleness;
   the untouched tenderness:
Two stone statues forever reaching,
   but never finding across a well-cut lawn:
That is its epitome.

                                           14 January 1979

Solitude
103

I do not wish to caress
    the coral of your breasts;
Cherry your lips;
Finger the mulberry nipples.

I do not want to smooth
    your sapling thighs
know the web of you again,
make your clitoris wetten,
Nor hear that sigh, halfcry.

These things, I want as a man.
But now, as a broken man,
As a child again,
I wish only to pay homage
    to your gentleness
To kneel at your feet,
    my head in your lap,
and cry and cry and cry.

                              20 January 1979

This is spiritual vandalism
When we piss into the chalice
or mumble a prayer we do not mean.

There is artistic vandalism
When we denigrate a Gaudier
    a Goya or deface
A Grinling Gibbons.

And there is emotional vandalism
When we take two hearts
   to make ourselves an omelette
and add a third to addle the other two.

21 January 1979

A Happy Poem

What is love?
It is what the shark feels
when the savage hook heads into its mouth
and, as it twists, the taut line shortens,
then as it swims away, the reel takes up the slack
till the fish feels the boat's side
And knows the bloody bludgeon of the savage gaffe.

What is love?
It is all in the waiting:
   for the telephone call which does not come,
Or, if made, is unanswered.

What is love?
It is anxiety: watching the clock
   when she is five minutes late;
Standing at the corner because you went there early.

What is love?
It is a deft pickpocket, a thief;
It is all sorrow, suffering and pain.
Love is not love, unless it is jealousy;
Love is not love, unless it is this grief.

21 January 1979

What is shame?
   It is when we learn to spell our name.

What is shame?
   It is when we find the coiled serpent
                   within our mind.

What is shame?
  It is our truth
Rust rotten, the eves our roof.

                          24 January 1979

Solitude
104

Your cruelty was you were so kind
   You stole my self and half my mind

Your cruelty was I trusted you
   as an Arab knows the sky is blue

Your cruelty was you took my heart
   and left me with no part, no part.

                          24 January 1979

Solitude
105

Come back to me
   as the leaves the trees;

Come back to me
   as the swallows dive;

Come back to me
   as the grass which grows;

Come back to me
   love that is love: it grows, it grows

                          24 January 1979

Solitude
106

Forget my anger
   which was love spurned,
love that lit; only half burned.

Forget my jealousy
   which was love spurned
love that lit; only half burned.

Forget my love
   which was self-conceit;
Find better food, enjoy the meat.

                          24 January 1979

Help me, dear God, to die
With less bitterness, resentment and strife
      as though I had enjoyed my life.

Help me, dear God, to pray:
Though on these shaky knees
I know you are not there,
      nor have I anything to say.

Help me, Dear God, to give you birth;
As a child, with straw for a manger,
As a child, with rags for a cot;
    Give me strength to give you life,
And bring hope to this Godless barren earth.

                           London, January 1979

Canto
II

There is a necessity for prayer,
I've found this in despair, in despair.
Knowing there is no God here, there or anywhere
But there is a necessity for prayer.

You do not need to kneel on a hassock,
Mumble a liturgy, it is not a plea for help from outside,
But the admission that there is no hope inside.

Prayer is a confession, a conversation
   between one part of one's mind and another,
   between your guilt and your remorse,
   between your regrets and the pain you've given,
   and the hurts you've not forgiven,
   between your selfish hopes and deserved disappointments,
   between the hate you dare not contemplate
   and the love you fear to remember.

There is a necessity for prayer,
Deny this, and you deny despair,
And if you're not bent with despair,
What gift of love or grace
   can reach you here, there or anywhere?

                               13 February 1979

Who is the I?

Arms across eyes, I stand; face against wall.
    The game: children steal up behind me.
I turn; any I see move; *'back to the start'*.
    Only those who are still may continue to tip-toe towards me;
The one who reaches me unobserved, thumps my shoulder:
    Wins the game, is me. So it is. I count five, turn.
Nobody is moving, but one: my name. She, back to the start.
    My name's not me. Who am I? Who will reach me,
Reveal my true identity?

Am I this pretty face? This presently perfect figure
    Inherited from ancestors, a link in chain of their survival?
'I saw you move. Back to the start.' Not me.
Or am I that past I try not to remember
That future I dare not imagine?

Is that little trowel, hook and gardening gloves, bottom of white
    cupboard
    In derelict kitchen, me; that asparagus bed, bundle of
    unplanted rose trees
Plonked in a bath?
    Those right-angled tears shed on so many railway platforms:
Before I found that to every goodbye there is an hello
    And to every hello, a goodbye, eventually,
While I play hop-scotch with my, and their, emotions?

Am I this groin, that groan so slight,
    A double backed beast feeding without appetite;
To be discarded: a moll, another doll?
    'I saw you move. Back to the start.'

Or am I my curiosity,
    My sharp mind blunted by education,
Leading only to the knowledge that we do not know?

Am I my vanity now so readily requited.
My competence which envy vilifies
My ambition which only disappointment can fill? *'Back to the start.'*

Or this duplicity, deception, self delusion and self love
    Able to justify, pretending justification is a reason.
Only myself from folly, fooled. *'They're closing in I see.'*

Is that white gate I painted, that cottage wall,
    That peat I hoed in here and there, my little, much loved garden over there
Where I planted rosemary now looking abandoned, a crucifix of care?
    Or are there spaghetti highways, those hamburger ads,
The whole vulgar syphilisation of the $, is this me where I belong,
    Or there, where only nettles and blackberries grow?
Someone is getting closer. I hear their tread.

Perhaps I am my fear? Fearing to become like that old discarded woman was
    Getting incontinent in a geriatric chair?
'The best pal you ever had' she'd said, before she herself no longer there.

Now a hand grasps my shoulder. This is my true identity.
    I am my flight. I am the hounds of my own despair
Persuing the hare I am: not found, not here, nor there.

                                                   19 March 1979

Canto III

Gamow's Big Bang and Bondi's Steady State theories
    can be reconciled
because both are correct, yet both inaccurate.

The big bang postulates an unique event;
   an absurd hypothesis in physics,
though not in theology.
                      Anything that is: must be
continuous, reversible or held by the scruff of the neck
   by time, which is a human concept,
mere convenience of measurement
   without meaning outside of clocks.
The belief in a big bang is the same thing
   as a belief in God,
with the not wholly defenceless proviso
   that His creation was both accidental
and purposeless.
   Essentially, it postulates: a start,
a beginning,
   but before the beginning
   there must be a before;
   and after the end, an end. . . .
Which thought makes the Duchess late for tea.
   True, the Doppler shift
indicates an expanding universe;
   K radiation suggests too
that this universe is the refuse from
   an explosion
which can reverberate, disperse,
   or like a spring, recoil
to an equilibrium,
   or more probably,
contract to a sink
from which it explodes again.

The essential fallacy
   is the notion that there is only one universe:
Hubble showed us there were innumerable more stars within this
      universe
some we can perceive, millions beyond light's sight;
What I am saying,
                without the mathematics to support,
only my night-light of intuition to show the way,
is: that there are as many universes
as there are stars.

    Indeed, each Black hole must be
a big bang in embryo:
                     each brat, a universe
born from a death, death from a birth
                     over and over, else time is God itself, –
the Duchess late for tea.

We say the speed of light is an absolute;
and mistake our measurement for meaning,
   which it has, in human terms alone.
But in physics the absolute is the point:
   the speed infers a time,
the time infers a clock.
    And just as nothing can overtake light
So, to pressure there's a point
   from which it cannot be contained and will release:
energy and matter are interchangeable,
   and light itself is only gravitation's footsteps,
Then it is obvious to me, if not explained to me
   that radiation, mass, matter, energy, call it
what you will,
               sink into that sink only to erupt again.

Not one universe but many,
              as many as counting means,
Or as Dante said: he did not know
              'death had undone so many.'
Like a boy's clay pipe with bubbles
         within the bubble,
Universes are being born all the time,
         which is not:
Creation is continuous or it could not have been, or be.

                                       30 March 1979

Canto
IV

Love is not a gift, but an achievement.
Not a commodity: something most need, seek
or imitate: thinking they have what they desire
because they believe they should desire it
only to find they are confined by the form, deprived of the
   content.

Love is not for all; not a rose, anyone can pick;
More a ruby, rare, dredged out of the sands of sorrow.
Can we all write the *Quintet in C Major*?
Perhaps that's what genius is: the capacity to love,
and why Schubert will bleed for ever?

Love not for beauty, for sex or pleasure;
Not in the tent in the bed, in the groin or the groan
from brief appetite. Not there, not there.
                              Nothing there.
But immediate casualness leading to ultimate disappointment.
   Not there.

Nor is love what we are given; but what we give,
When not reciprocated. It flowers only
When we forgive, when we make the scars of our suffering
heal the wounds of our sorrow;
When we keep the door open which was shut on us;
and feel for him, or her, who supplanted us;
when we like her for her faults or failings
those uglinesses we are beneath each other's skins.

Love is when we nurse that child,
   aware it is not ours, or theirs, but what we are.

Love is something I have sought but never given.
How then can I be loved, be forgiven?

                                        March 1979

Canto
V

When we are young, old age is a period
   we do not think about,
it is a taboo like death; and
   those about us who are old
receive little sympathy, even ridiculed by us;
Then later, much later, we become slowly aware
   this abyss confronts us too only to find then
that what we have already encloses us:
that our only future is our past;
that our hopes evaporated, our memories corroded, unreliable or
   painful;
that we are discarded, impotent, unable
invalids without having experienced sickness
sitting alone, dining alone, sleeping alone
   a telephone our life-line,
a paperback novel, our only constant companion.

We are surrounded by our possessions
   we no longer value,
books we wish we had not written;
having achieved recognition,
   long after ambition left us;
Perhaps even acclaimed for things we regret having done;
Alone, sometimes wealthy but wanting nothing,
bankrupt of companionship,
missing those friends whose friendship we did not cultivate;
or grieving for ourselves over those who have died before us;
Then we decide to fight back: we take up yoga
eat yoghurt or bran,
cut down on smoking, with a stick
   go for a walk without a destination,
   to return to a room comfortably furnished
with uncomfortable mementos,
   and the little time that's left

   drags its slippered heels;
     or we take to a hobby, fretwork, jigsaw or raffia;
At our worst, do good.

1 April 1979

Canto VI

Hope

What is it but hope
   which lifts our batlike sails
till billowed with that breeze
   they lift our sullen prow
to erase, to scrub the surf behind us?

Only hope can flight the linnet's wing,
   give the panther stealth,
the lanky heron patience
or buzzard the hawk
over the gorse and bracken cliff.

Whose hand but hope's hand
   takes love's first blind embrace?
Whose eyes but hope's eyes
   seek and see her return
While I have life left,
   not a cup of ash, which burned?

What kneels the vicar in his empty church
   or makes him preach a faith he doubts himself
In the pew of night, abandoned?

How does the ungainly dancer
   persevere, the ungifted painter
Spoil another canvas, or makes this writer
   reach for another page of pain?

Does hope nest an invisible silver feathered bird
    within the magnolia's cup, and there
lay its unseen eggs
    to hatch, to fly,
butterflies emblazoned with wings
    of amethyst and crimson
over velvet lawns, where light itself
    pauses to gaze upon the grace of flight.

Is it the keel of my despair
    and if not there, sorrow not here, not there?
Is it the shimmering oasis, vain mirage
    in the desert, the sands of oblivion, of ambition?

Is hope not a disease, virus of vanity
    innoculating mediocrity
making the poor impervious to poverty,
    the rich immune to the burden of their wealth?
Is hope not hopeless, while we have hope?
And our only hope, the abandoning of hope, completely?

                                    25 April 1979

Canto VII

Faith

Faith, a fugitive, hounded by reason
    Scampering to warren hope, burrow of belief.
Belief measured with fear holding one end of tape,
    terror the other, the measurement, delusion.

Faith, buttonhole we have got, those without,
    misguided and mistaken,
A quadratic without equations, a formula
    without components,
The solution which ignores the problem,
    Answers, by evading question.

Faith, the branch we cling to
  on the tree which is not there
But in our mind, and those who seek to sever it
  are to us profane, and to themselves a life quite blind.

It curtains caution, prods courage to destruction,
  thumbscrews cruelty,
It makes vandals of us all.
Allowing Torquemada to kneel devout,
  Stalin and Himmler stand about
Both fingering a rosary, each bead marked with common good.
It vultures the empty sky impatient for us to die;
  Then with slobbering beak drops promptly
To receive our souls and pick our bones quite dry.

Faith, is the sapphire I have sought
  within the sands, the desert of my thought
Scrubbing through the dustbin of my days
  finding nothing but a fag-end there.
Now too hopeless to seek further
  or pretend to have found other ways.

                                              30 April 1979

Canto VIII

Happiness

'Why don't you ever write anything happy?' she once asked
  who had herself given most happiness to me.
And I had not replied then.
  Perhaps because when we have what we desire
We do not know it, or value it, until deprived of it;
  Or because we are happy by being unaware
And can only recall that joy, when we despair?

But because she challenged me,
  I will pick up her pretty glove
And lark these words so that she
  and all the world will know, if not in my time,

  then in hers, what it was she gave to me
   before, from fear of losing her, I drove her from me –
At least for a time, if I have that time
  before I burn, or she returns to me.

First, she yielded her eyes, her lips, then chose
  to undress her loveliness, to disclose her thighs' mouth
As gracefully as a flame of the forest grows,
  and after, taking me to herself and her satiety,
She lay her head on my shoulder
  light as a white rose lies on the evening;
Next, how she would request the repeat
  'her aperitif', if my maimed mind dare recall
How often? How often? All joy in that one question.

Next, how she shared, milked pleasure from simple things:
  the white washed wall, she hooked, the poisoned nettle beds,
The black velvet coat, the grouse, the squid,
  and how happiness flowered in her eyes
When that lobster pot contained a lobster
  which we had caught, which we alone had caught,
Which we now shared as we both shared each other –
  we, who now live apart,
Each with only half a heart.

But to hold her glove above my inert head,
  I'll force the remnants of my mind to recall that happiness
  because I know they're not beyond recall.
There was that image of her with Fenice at her feet,
  and Donizetti at her elbow;
There was that pink dress completed; those little pearls first
  worn;
  six years of unnumbered meetings leaves
Without a branch wind to quarrel from.
Careful meals, innumerable, silvered gifts,
  cuddles invariable,
Devotion, friendship and passion; and over all
  those little things; the chocolate by my bed
which now Leviathans, Titanics in my head.

But happiness is a swallow
   caught or pinned against the wall:
No swallow, then no bird at all. Happiness is in being,
   and it seems to me we are happiest only when unaware,
Unconscious of what we hold,
   there's the pity, my larks wings can't unfold
And words are worthless:
   only her eyes could speak
The poetry beyond my pen, my flight.

Or is it, yet, it is, the hope that what we are to one another,
   must in time be realized
When you bolt that door with forgiveness
   and aware of what we had
Hide it from all the world except ourselves
   to sapphire your eyes again.

Perhaps dearest, happiness is an almond blossom
   which remembered fruits and then, as sorrow, falls?
For me, happiness is you. This swallow grasses here.

                              29 April 1979

Canto
IX

Grief

Grief is not death's demesne
   not the solitary mourner by the slotted grave
Where the two ropes hang on which the box is laid
   nor is it the pale soles of the strickeneds' feet
Kneeling beside the pyre with ghee upon his head,
   the sickly smell of sandlewood
Smoking from well stoked fire,
Grief is not these, perhaps remorse instead.

Grief is not the tolling of the leaden bell,
   the slow marched gravelled tread, the muffled drum,

Stallion saddled riderless, flag half-masted,
   neither in velvet drapes nor behind those eyes
Swollen with self pity
   after the will is read;
Grief is not death's demesne
   there it cannot rent or sit.
The mind accepts eviction
   when life is beyond recall
In this, death's merciful, is for ourselves, or feigned.

Where then does it serpent?
   what cobra it?
What makes it's quick spite so slow yet so certain
   without an antidote, but we turn adder too
Tempted to damage him or her
   with suicide, camouflaged revenge,
Murder by one remove, spiteful, pitiless, though pitiful?

No, grief lords it elsewhere
   Squires the manor there,
And in this vaulted hall,
   lonely, if not alone;
   solitary, not knowing solitude,
An unrequited vigil, waiting
   for someone who does not come
Except in dreams; a silent waltz
   without a beat, a waiting to wake to a tidy sheet;
Embrace of unconsciousness,
   consciousness of defeat.

Grief tenants it elsewhere,
  is High Sheriff, there
He lives where love is, or was,
   and with an unrelenting, tireless gait
Stalks the unending of his state,
   punctual with remorse,
   only regret, not late,
   each day, a little death
   each wreath, punishment

> Without remission
>   unable to forgive the sin
> He alone committed,
>   unable to forget that love,
> She, dear child, admitted
>   love of that high order:
> That is what grief is.

1 May 1979

Canto
X

Jealousy

Jealousy is the proof of love, they tell me.
   But of which kind of love I ask?
Of jealousy I have known enough, enough,
   Because I did not love enough, enough.

If she whom I love was loved
   because I looked upon her as a thing to be possessed,
denying her own being, her nature, its expression,
   then better for her that I were dispossessed
Whatever the consequence to me of my suppression.

Jealousy corrodes, rusts us all: makes us small
   to ourselves, minimal,
till we hate ourself more than our rival,
   reducing us to self-pity, pitiful:
self-contempt we cannot contemplate:
   a mirror insulting our imagined image,
damaging our esteem, built-in illusion and smug dream.

If we love – oh, where is that rare butterfly
   which flaunts its crimson wings
or linnets the pavillioned sky and sings and sings? –
   then surely, we must love her for her wholeness,
the holiness of her being?

Do we resent the rain
   because it falls on other's fields, but ours?
The wind which harps other's trees?
   Do we cry out: blow on me, or not at all?
What kind of love is this, I ask?

And the answer is:
   it is the kind of love you gave, you knew:
Not enough, enough – how few, so few; not you, not you
   have climbed that cliff where love stands naked dressed in mist,
   caressed by hail and gale –
You worm, you have not learned your alphabet,
   and poet that you are,
You remain emotionally illiterate;
   may your last years mole you:
Back to your bench.
   Learn from the dragon fly or finch which amethysts the stream,
   or flits from wall to wall;
Back to your bench:
   unlearn all that you knew:
know, too late,
   admit your inability to love at all:
it is not love, to love at lower rate.

So put away your pen; find humility;
   Your arrogance has undone you.
Swear now: never to write again:
   You've bled, misled, enough;
Let silence alone speak your sorrow,
   Tell them to read your tears to laugh;
And open your hands
   So she may fly away.

Would you rein back the waves,
   comb the spray's wild mane,
tether the tide, halter the wind,
   or shear the clouds tangled fleece?
No, enough's, enough, enough.

                                                 11 May 1979

Canto XI

Forgiveness

I, who had backed the black,
   watched the wheel spin,
To see the ball fall
          repeatedly for me,
then rake in my stakes in spite of the pain I'd caused,
   now saw the red come up surprisingly
when I'd put all. Bankrupt, I could not take
   the losses I have often caused others,
and had now been given.

Reduced, abandoned, beggared
   Cringeing in the gutter of my days,
I held out my palm
         for the bread of her eyes,
To see her pass me by,
              and my lips cursed her,
Though my blood blessed her.

So I crawled to a priest and said:
   'Should I forgive?'
'Yes', he replied.
          'I lied: I've tried, I've tried' I cried,
'So tell me how, how do we forgive?
   Where does this jewel He gave, hide?
What day clenches this diamond's ray?
Which rock can reveal these amethysts I have sought
   within the steppes, the deserts of my thought?
Why must such an opal secret itself from me,
   Yet sapphire the bull frog's head
   or emerald the panther's wild eye?
Why can't I find in all this barren land
   the one jewel I seek to put upon her hand?
So tell me, not that I should forgive, but how, how?'

And this simple old man shook his head.
  'You are too clever for me to teach you anything' he said,
'But all I know is this:
              the wish to forgive,
                Is all there is to forgiveness'.
I grabbed this poor man's wealth,
  byzantium bereft by comparison.
So wear this invisible ring, and fear not,
  it was not I who gave it you,
But He who had garnets scratch across his brow
And rubies drip from both His hard sand feet.

                            13 May 1979

Canto
XII

It is an occupied country
  where I live,
at least, in part; imprisoned,
In a concentration camp;
  in solitary confinement,
bereft of everything except my heart.

My cell is as high as I am tall;
  if I lie down on the floor,
My feet touch one wall, my head, the other;
  There is a bucket for excreta
And my thoughts. An electronic eye
  monitors my movements:
Suicide, a privilege, not encouraged:
  a remission, remote: unlikely to be earned.
Every half hour the warder
  Opens a small shutter or prison door:
We stare into each others' eyes, vacantly.

Most of the day, I sit upon the board which is my bed,
    ravaged by memories, the past I can't forget,
Trying to undo what I did, and unsay what I said:
    An unending fatigue, that will not let me go:
Shackled by regret to regret; tortured, without a torturer;
ravaged by hounds which have no scent or bark,
Till cornered by the truth, I stand to raise my fist
    Against those vultures which carrion my mind,
Only to find they are not there:
    that prison is anywhere I am:
In this stalag of remorse.

                            14 May 1979

Canto XIII

He who has not been tempted to take his own life
    Has not lived at all,
At least, not fully.
    For it is not possible to love completely,
    Without giving yourself entirely;
To be dependant on; to love is to become
    not in oneself, but in another:
A grave security risk, a wallet for any pickpocket
    to pick up; an unguarded stall; shoplifter's dream rifled by any thief.
And to love as we loved is, at the loss, all grief:
    a grief which will not die itself
nor wilt, forgotten as a casual wreath.

And just as two spots from the same laser
    shew bright and dark interference fringes
where waves of light
reinforce or cancel each other,
    and prove that light plus light makes darkness
when their two oscillations are tripped up out of step,

So with us who rode so high, to be brought down so low,
till the beam of light we were,
   makes night itself irridescent and aglow.

So here, in this shadow of a shadow, my mind decides
   to do it,
My hand reaches out
   to undo it;
To put this burden down I can no longer carry,
   weighing more than I weigh myself.
As I clench the drug, relief alleviates
   my kneeled despair;
And death waits as a friend,
   who promised to be there.

But slowly sadly, I put the unopened bottle down again
   because I fear that my grief might cause her grief,
And doubt that these two waves of darkness
   would shed any light
however shuffled. Though the lack of her is night, is night, is
   night.

Anyhow suicide's impossible;
   for without her,
I have in truth, if not in fact,
   breathed in my death and already died.

19 May 1979

Solitude
107

If time is motion
Why does it drag while I am still?

If time has only one dimension
how has it such weight, such volume
now she is not here?

If time is the sequence of events
why have I no future, but my past
when all of space is filled by absence
and only what is not, is real?

         May 1979

Since the present is invisible
 because light loiters
Making only the past apparent,
 is not my future equally obscure;
And why I am not aware of any tense
 but her past presence and
 present abscence?

         May 1979

Canto XIV
Ambition

Ambition, an horizon,
 unobtainable, receeding as we approach it;
A mirage, oasis to which we trudge
 through the deserts of our years,
to stand bereft, rucksack of disappointment;
 or at its best, reached after thirst, quenched;
Knowing that what we had sought, was not our seeking;
What we have bought, not worth our buying.

To mask the innocence which all children wear
 to hide immediate greed, ultimate despair,
Is as an auction:
 at which they put their vanity up for sale,
Then bid against themselves, to raise the price,
 only to find they are both vendor and purchaser,
And as the hammer falls,
 they're left holding their fakes,
having to pay the full commission.

For a painter, recognition comes, if it comes at all,
Long after he has ceased to value those who praise him or collect
 him.
The bust is not tardy: late, too late.
For scientists, their search for knowledge
 reached only when they know they have none.
For politicians: power, when power is all contempt;
They find that between politics and prostitution,
 the elder profession, the more honourable.
For the lawyer, every law's a tart:
 willing to enact any obscenity for payment at the start.
To the Judge: no justice, only mercy.
To the Priest: no faith, only doubts,
 the belief that he is being conned,
Has conned; he finally kneels because he hasn't got a leg to stand
 on.

For woman: the most beautiful, most damned:
   they set their sights upon themselves
to find that men are not looking at them,
   but regard them; their ambition or vanity
fulfilled with cruel brevity, with spite,
   replacing appetite. Those, once called lovely:
dismissed or damned with praise, hospitable or being kind.

For the poet, who had only words to work with,
   he, poor dolt, has only words to end with:
a pitiful babble,
   he runs his hand through his greying hair,
picks over his remaindered books,
   knowing ambition was a delusion, a metaphor
without truth, without tense, without meaning:
   a joke, not in the best of taste,
That all his life was verbiage, vain waste.

                                      10 June 1979

Canto
XV

From The Shallows (For C.33)

You from the depths; I, from the shallows.
Both guilty of the same crime: arrogance.
Justly condemned. Each imprisoned
   in ourselves; sentenced without remission.

In our narrow cells we crumbed
   similar conclusion:
'Domine, non sum dignus'.
   Unloved, we know
Nobody is worthy to be loved:
   'Domine, non sum dignus'.

At exercise, we marched with the same lags
Neither of us recognized any at first,
   But after a time, through our unshed tears we saw

Behind Suffering stood Sorrow
And behind Sorrow stood Love
   and holding that hand, grief.
In for a stretch, our companions:
   suffering, a pickpocket, sorrow, a thief.

Both of us slowly discovering
   that it is only when the world has taken everything from you,
You have anything worth having at all,
   or are anybody yourself.
All men are humans; few, beings too.
   Most people are understudies,
In parts, we wrote: they enact,
   their thoughts, were ours
their lives were ours,
   even their passion, a quotation
their love, plagiarism or pretence:
   Life at one remove,
At liberty without identity
   never having stood naked in suffering
to dress in the rags of sorrow;
   that our privilege (or arrogance):
A raiment, our invisible visitor wore.

He, who makes Hamlet as superficial
   and frivolous as Malvalio;
And by comparison, all Greek Tragedy, a farce.
He whom you know understood the leprosy of the leper;
   the shame that was yours, the remorse that is mine;
Who perceived the darkness of the blind
   And the light, darker than darkness, of the prigs
Who are unkind, who live from vanity to achieve ambitions or
   pleasure,
Who are bankrupt with their wealth,
   never suffering, being insensitive to the pain they cause,
have caused, knowing our self justification.

He, on whom the virtuous rely,
   who turned to the woman taken in adultery, to say
'Her sins are forgiven her because she loved much',
He whose ultimate passion, birthed compassion

    with his shoddy little supper in a cheap cafe
       betrayed; for silver, identified by a kiss,
inevitably a kiss,
       then denied by him on whom he had relied,
thought devoted. His agony in the garden,
       his friends sleeping while he wept.

Then his final humiliation:
       Justice, without mercy,
Washing its hands, then stringing him up:
       A King crowned with thorns,
Nails in his hands, nails in his feet,
       Gall to his cracked lips
While soldiers diced for his clothes
       Oblivious of those two women weeping.
He, who accepted:

who knew that all passion was passion
       and that good and evil are identified
with only repentence, yours, mine or theirs
       to separate or redeem.

'Let him who has not sinned throw the first stone'
It was, as you said C.33, worth living to have said that.
And as we both know it is worth being imprisoned
       to value that. Sorrow alone
Enables, sorrow is all of art. As Schubert said:
'All I have written, I have written from my sorrow'
Both you and I could not say more than that.
Now I will weep, you will shed my tears: in humility.
We are the same man: there is only one man.

                                       15 June 1979

Solitude
108

Value me no less
    because I am yours

1979

Solitude
109

It is when we feel that we have been betrayed
That we ourselves betray;
When we are wounded, wound:
To make bleed where we have bled.
The hurts we receive should never
    let us grieve; the pain we were given
must be forgiven; not as a gift,
a spiritual gratuity, but as a right
to her who hurt as we hurt her:
It is when we salve our bruises that we bruise.
What strength we have, what thought we can find
Should meditate on the pain we caused, and cause;
All else is maudlin self pity,
    the reeling drunk with an unrepentant mind.

1979

Nature is no consolation:
>> the daffodils remind;
the primroses smirk, even the crocuses
>> sport pink and yellow ridicule.

My great gaunt cliffs
>> steeped with bracken
and indifference; acres of pasture, green,
>> callous and bare;
forests of firewood: everywhere,
>> you not there.

The whole universe
>> meaningless to me;
Light itself now loiters; doppler shifts to vacuity;
>> From things no comfort, love alone means.

>> 1979

date unknown

Solitude
110

With silent wings
I circle round your silence;
On timeless feet
I walk towards your absence;
Behind closed eyes
I look upon your presence.

Lullaby

Oh when will the encircling bird of sleep
Alight on my eyelids and let me creep
Into the fastness of its folded wings,
Oh, when will this elusive linnet nest?

Nocturne

In the centre of his brain
   floats a red anemone;
petals of, protruding through
   harvest of her hair;
Fold the petals, press the brain:
   Here's seed from it.

The Magnolia

From where these birds
   which perch upon the bough
Leafless, but for their white wings
   Of ivory or alabaster
Now furled, so spruce, so still?
   What dark wind swept them?
Across which seas?
   Drawn by what instinct?
Migrating from where to where?
   Or are these not birds, nor flowers,
But hands in prayer
   clenched in brief hope
Wrung with long despair?

Index of First Lines and Titles

Titles of Poems are in Italic

A Ballad p. 94
A Canticle for Briony p. 101
A flock of flamingoes p. 182
A Friend p. 284
A happy poem p. 315
A jungle (S) p. 201
A lost demented nomad, he misspent his life p. 294
A Mr William Gaskill said (P) p. 197
A navvy with hobnail boots, p. 311
A Syllogism, p. 176
A Woman of fashion p. 282
A Woman sleeping on a train p. 281
Acceleration is absolute; speed (US) p. 241
Across the desert p. 21
After dinner Speech, p. 15
Ah well! all these sailors p. 42
Air Raid p. 62
All right, run off with you and go (S) p. 129
Ambition, an horizon (C) p. 338
Ambition Canto p. 338
An old man widdling down his leg p. 301
And he reached that point (S) p. 164
And this evening, as the sun p. 81
Any man might miss (S) p. 128
Appenato p. 87
Aria p. 8
Arms across eyes, I stand face against wall p. 319
As a baker, he went from house to house p. 209
As April perches on winter branches (S) p. 214
As a goldfish in a bowl (LL) p. 266
As a hand, the glove, the pelt, the hare (LL) p. 265
As thrush, lark and linnet are (S) p. 136

As wet lilac bruised with scent (S) p. 120
At 18 they are as Asia p. 153
Ascension p. 89
At the thrust of the stiff spring, oh la p. 50
At twenty you were the distraction p. 103
At Windsor where the castle keep p. 59
Atlantic death waits (LL) p. 263
Aubade p. 51
Autumn like a pheasant's tail p. 114
Autumn pheasants the hedge (LL) p. 262
Autumn shawls the hill p. 226
Autumn p. 230
Ballad Of Stratton Gaol p. 55
Barnstaple p. 290
Be well advised (P) p. 195
Because a lady asks me (S) p. 215
Because I enjoy a solitary tree p. 8
Because I have looked into your eyes (S) p. 122
Because my eyes have stared (S) p. 131
Because of night (LL) p. 260
Beside these bougainvilleas, Gandhi fell p. 176
Black earth whites her bones p. 285
Both my fingers and the calendar (LL) p. 256
Briony p. 79
But when we forgive (S) p. 303
Butterfly dreams unfurl p. 296
By starred, violet tranquillity (LL) p. 265
By this bed, in this vase p. 250
Canon For Three Critics p. 95
Canticle p. 174
Canzone p. 36
Canzone: The River p. 3
Carol ('This Song's to a girl') p. 85
Carol ('Where the earth Floor was puddled with urine;') p. 151
Child, who birthed a gentle June p. 295
Christ, is this thy cross, tossed p. 67
Clasp For A Mislaid Necklace p. 146
Come back to me (S) p. 316
Come to me, Death (S) p. 168
Come to me promptly p. 251
Confessio Amantis p. 7
Confound Tennessee Williams (P) p. 198
Confound your jealousy (S) p. 181
Cotehele, p. 298
Damn and blast the middle classes (P) p. 190

Damn and blast you (S) p. 112
Dansa p. 50
Danse Macabre p. 1
Dartmoor p. 67
Dear friends, be kind, abandon me p. 220
Dearest, be kind (S) p. 303
Dearest, be ruthless (S) p. 130
Dearest, do me a favour (S) p. 124
Dearest, I have an admission to make (S) p. 291
Dearest, in the autumn of my years (LL) p. 265
Dearest, it is no longer true (S) p. 118
Dearest, promise to be merciful to me now (S) p. 299
Dearest, since I cannot say why I love you (S) p. 120
Dearest, your absence (S) p. 304
Death be more proud (US) p. 242
Death said: why do you fear me? p. 277
Dirge p. 301
Do me a favour, treat me with contempt (S) p. 109
Do not believe I loved you (S) p. 293
Do not believe the truth p. 258
Do what Rimbaud did eh p. 14
Doctors are mere moles (P) p. 193
Does summer p. 229
Does the terror or the tiger's tooth p. 68
Does the wind move the branches (S) p. 123
Drink! For the night is flowing like black wine p. 88
Drinking Song p. 88
Easter Lullaby p. 100
Easter: two days after p. 133
Egypt a nation with only its past before it p. 288
Elegant, immaculately turned out p. 282
Ethel Duncan, p. 287
Envoi p. 179
Epigram p. 16
Epilogue p. 121
Epitaph p. 287
Epitaph for Milne (P) p. 255
Epitaph For A Friend p. 309
Epitaph On An Unknown Passenger p. 91
Epitaph For R. D. I p. 116
Epitaph for R. D. II. p. 116
Epitaph For Sir Mike Ansell p. 183
Epithalmium p. 165
Excuse me, forgive me if I interrupt p. 148
Experiment With Old Metaphors p. 33

Faith, a fugitive, hounded by reason (C) p. 326
Faith Canto p. 326
Feast of Sowing p. 35
Flotsam p. 67
For A Dying Woman p. 155
For A Growing Girl p. 283
For A Young Man, Aged 90 p. 59
For an old reason p. 29
For Continuity p. 6
For length: a ruler; for weight, a balance p. 187
For Sir Francis Chichester's return p. 166
For what jasmin of gentleness p. 280
Forget my anger (S) p. 317
Forgive my talent p. 211
Forgiveness Canto p. 333
Franz Schubert p. 309
From The Shallows (C) p. 339
From where these birds p. 345
From where this crimson p. 224
Galoshered, shuffling up the street p. 276
Gamow's Big Bang and Bondi's steady (C) p. 320
Give me your hand p. 23
Great souls in prison cells lie p. 55
Greedy Earth, who now devours my own mother p. 285
Grief Canto p. 329
Grief is not death's demesne (C) p. 329
Grief is not something we give the dead p. 301
Had We The Time p. 5
Handkerchiefs are the vultures (S) p. 157
Happiness Canto p. 327
Having descended the escalator p. 91
Hay Harvest Song p. 34
He did not travel up the Amazon p. 221
He kneels to his God p. 271
He was a man of such considerable promise p. 116
He was a man with a handsome, wounded face p. 267
He was neither prince nor politician p. 65
He who has not been tempted to take his own life (C) p. 335
Help me, dear God, to die p. 317
Her birthday – up she gets, she's twenty three p. 28
Her moss of sleep upon the bark of night (S) p. 119
Here Igor and Ez lie beneath their eiderdown of stone p. 295
Here is a rose p. 182
Here lies my mother p. 287
Here, where the modest water flows p. 155

Here's Milne: his feet cushions to his skull p. 255
Here's the ground she and I, let our p. 146
Hope Canto p. 325
How can we be parted (S) p. 144
How eloquent her leaf gentle eyes are (S) p. 212
How fragile this frightened sparrow is (S) p. 141
How leaf we are (S) p. 150
How leaf we are; these autumn years p. 297
How snails the year (LL) p. 262
Huge cliffs shoulder the sea. You can p. 1
Husband! p. 47
I am as hungry as the wind p. 132
I am dying p. 293
I am going where p. 274
I am kneeling in the chapel of Saint Simon p. 58
I am nothing, if not honest (S) p. 168
I can remember my mother's womb p. 6
I do not wish to caress (S) p. 314
I had hoped that (S) p. 163
I have at last come to terms (S) p. 123
I have come back again (S) p. 222
I have now become grateful for my worries (S) p. 173
I know what it is I seek in you (S) p. 201
I put my hand into my pocket (P) p. 191
I ride, the road winds uphill (S) p. 170
I sit alone (LL) p. 253
I sit in an empty room, so crowded (US) p. 249
I spoke to my sadness and I said (S) p. 133
I stepped out into the dark p. 268
I turned in time to see a star, stretch p. 11
I, who had backed the black (C) p. 333
I who had sound health and a wife p. 42
I wish to ask you a question p. 154
I wonder if her wise, wide eyes p. 25
I worry how to tell my love p. 24
I would that my love should grow p. 172
I'm a psychic patient p. 113
I'm as blind as a bat p. 95
Iago should have been a woman as (US) p. 246
If cities could speak p. 186
If gratitude is prayer p. 174
If he were to walk into this cafe p. 156
If his love is all possessive p. 273
If I could rid myself of myself p. 255
If I were a Prince (S) p. 105

If only you had three breasts (P) p. 204
If our ability to love (S) p. 142
If pheasant's head (C) p. 234
If sleep is the way p. 287
If there's a life after death (P) p. 192
If they should ask where he found beauty (S) p. 180
If they should ask you (S) p. 227
If this manoeuvring is love (S) p. 275
If those rodents who've gnawed or ignored p. 297
If time is motion (S) p. 336
If you could see my hand (LL) p. 254
If you had died (S) p. 164
Impromptu For A Child p. 79
If you persist in concentrating on p. 133
In a blind world of grass p. 83
In a six-cylinder fury p. 48
In England, honours come (P) p. 194
In Memoriam ('Here Igor and Ez lie beneath their eiderdown of stone) p. 295
In Memoriam ('She said: 'One of the advantages when you're about to die is:') p. 208
In my time, I was here too (S) p. 158
In the centre of his brain p. 345
In Delhi p. 176
In Dublin p. 177
In the forest of my dreams p. 121
In the morning, I am sad (5) p. 233
Inscription For A Drawing, p. 225
Insignificance p. 11
Instead Of Mobile Worker p. 113
Instructions At My Death p. 225
Is life, this life, his life p. 226
Isn't there something in common p. 33
It is an occupied country (C) p. 334
It is early May (LL) p. 256
It is essential that an ultimatum should be sent p. 15
It is May: still days p. 220
It is of woman's love I sing p. 3
It is when we feel that we have been betrayed (S) p. 342
It rains behind my eyes (S) p. 165
It was as if I'd met the Lord p. 7
It was not that I raised myself to Him p. 89
It's all very disappointing, most disappointing (S) p. 126
Jasmine lies as gently on the evening air p. 57
Jealousy Canto p. 331

Jealousy is the proof of love, they tell me (C) p. 331
Jou-Jou p. 20
Just as an unmined ruby (S) p. 233
Just as I used (S) p. 115
Just as the same square-winged buzzard suddenly hunts p. 160
Just as the spring in tiny primroses speaks (US) p. 242
Justice? What's Justice? Did Jesus or Pilate (US) p. 240
Keats trod here p. 230
Knowing that a cock or bull p. 16
Lament for Ben, p. 226
Larks are the Sparks p. 93
Last night I dreamt (S) p. 188
Last night, my knees searched for you p. 131
Leaf that I am (S) p. 117
Legend from Vancouver p. 178
Lenin, having forgotten his aims (P) p. 190
Let me lie at the cliff edge p. 225
Let us start here: for this, is where we are p. 35
Let's speak around and about yesterday p. 21
Life's easy for her p. 4
Lightly as willow (S) p. 118
Like a waterfall of wind p. 79
Like little clouds on a green sky, my sheep p. 79
Like skulls, with all their fears still there p. 62
Lines For My Daughter On Her Wedding Day p. 182
Lines For N.S.'s First Birthday p. 149
Lines Written By My Mother's Bed p. 251
Lines Written For A Wine Merchant's Christmas Card p. 85
Little girl p. 269
Lobes of mauve lilac p. 135
Loneliness is our thirst (S) p. 122
Looney's Song p. 30
Lord Jesus once was a p. 100
Love is in the loving (S) p. 157
Love is not a gift, but an achievement (C) p. 323
Love like a dog barks at the heal of my leisure p. 36
Love like a storm breaks (S) p. 180
Love passes, grief does not (S) p. 171
Lullaby ('Oh when will the encircling bird of sleep') p. 344
Lullaby ('Sleep, My Baby') p. 161
Lullaby ('What falls more lightly') p. 152
Madam, if you are unaware (S) p. 124
Marriage is mutual cannabilism (P) p. 197
Marriage is nothing more than loneliness (US) p. 243
May this rose p. 210

Mike Ansell p. 277
Mr Eliot informed me that he was convinced (P) p. 192
Mr Harold Wilson says (P) p. 196
Mr Holy Ghost p. 11
Mr Pensamiento p. 64
Most people are unhappy (S) p. 125
Moto Perpetuo p. 81
Mountains are merciless as man (S) p. 135
München-Gladbach Lyric p. 134
Murderers are merciful to me (S) p. 106
Music's no food, Olivia, it's a poison (S) p. 299
Must I, who've searched so long for her (S) p. 206
My health is going; my time, almost gone (US) p. 247
My heart burns away slowly p. 64
My mind mothed by jealousy (S) p. 306
My unkind heart, take pity on my heart (US) p. 243
My unhappiness has become a second skin to me (S) p. 163
My unhappiness now crystallizes (US) p. 245
Nature is no consolation p. 343
Neither health nor happiness (S) p. 200
Night creeps p. 32
Night like a lean leopard p. 17
No Easter egg, my child p. 252
No logical contradiction p. 102
Nocturne p. 345
Not for her beauty: that could be replaced p. 212
Not in the swing of the year p. 15
Notes of a dream p. 84
Nothing unique can, or could, exist p. 221
Noticing that one of our randy guns p. 41
Now I mast high (S) p. 207
Now my glad eyes butterfly and rise p. 302
Now palms my hands above my sleepless eyes (U) p. 266
Now sap squirts p. 275
Now silks the yellow on the daffodil (LL) p. 264
Now that we love (S) p. 119
Now that our love by life has been betrayed (S) p. 138
Now the East Wind p. 102
Now wolf grief throats remorse p. 272
Oblivion as a writer (S) p. 183
Oh bugger this. At this rate p. 231
Oh earth, I am in love with thee p. 22
Oh, I wish I were an orange tree p. 61
Oh my god with what agility (S) p. 49
Oh my love, I am as lonely p. 87

Oh Rose Marie as you are my love p. 51
Oh rose of sorrow p. 96
Oh shall I sing of Josephine p. 94
Oh when will the encircling bird of sleep p. 344
Old bottles on an old shelf contain p. 85
Omar Cayenne p. 210
On Summer p. 302
On wings of thought p. 210
Only because you ask me, will I write (S) p. 209
Only the deaf dare listen to Schubert p. 311
Our difficulty is p. 23
Our grief is not for his death p. 158
Our urchin love was brief (S) p. 168
Ovid was driven from his home (LL) p. 253
The Panther p. 17
Parish Church p. 12
Pastorale p. 268
Passion's no prince p. 17
Per Piazzale Roma; Alla Ferrovia; Per Piazza San Marco p. 296
Phallic Song I p. 29
Phallic Song II p. 32
Pheasants' feathers of amethyst p. 270
Poem in a Painting (Solitude, 6) p. 105
Poem Written At The Request Of A Political Group p. 148
Poems From The War I p. 41
Poems From The War II p. 42
Piesport p. 227
Plain Song p. 24
Platform Postcard p. 218
Plymouth p. 300
Poem ('In a six-cylinder fury') p. 48
Poem ('Not in the swing of the year') p. 15
Poet 1937 ('The maddening traffic of my dreams') p. 19
Poetry p. 187
Postcard ('Today the Vicar came down – it being Good Friday,–') p. 31
Postcard ('When all this place is rubble, ash and dross') p. 140
Post Script p. 221
Practical Ballad I p. 82
Practical Ballad II p. 83
Question p. 14
Rampant lion haunches, fells the evening (LL) p. 264
Remember me p. 218
Requiem p. 231
Rider, rein up your horse, let it graze p. 183

Rondo 'La Clemenza di Ito' p. 293
What am I? This name p. 205
Rogo Ergo Sum p. 205
Saints go to considerable lengths (P) p. 194
Schubert p. 185
Searching for his anima p. 116
Seascape p. 273
September shawls the shoulder of the year p. 230
Sheaves of grass p. 34
She bore a son p. 271
She lies propped up by pillows p. 155
She possesses me completely p. 140
She said of the advantages when p. 208
She, who in my heart (S) p. 189
She, who's my music p. 132
Since nothing of itself can be p. 165
Since she whom I love p. 139
Since the present is invisible p. 337
Single Ticket p. 274
Sleep blackbirds and bears p. 312
Sleep, my baby p. 161
Snapshot p. 114
Some people don't like the rain. I like the rain p. 83
Song ('I am kneeling in the Chapel of Saint Simon,') p. 58
Song ('Larks are the sparks') p. 93
Song ('Sooner or later, you') p. 26
Song ('The clean shy leaves undress the trees') p. 26
Song Of The Earth p. 22
Song To Sea p. 33
Sooner or later, you p. 26
Sorry, no Easter egg p. 252
Spanish Song p. 47
Spring p. 275
Spring Song p. 182
Spring is no certain thing p. 20
Spring's first enthusiasm fades p. 47
St Thomas Aquinas wrote (P) p. 191
Stables: A national trust shop p. 298
Strong as the Nelson Column and with no pigeons on it p. 32
Strophe and Anti-Strophe at Bakerloo p. 63
Summer ('What is Summer') p. 57
Summer ('Does Summer') p. 229
Taller than his shadow: a man p. 277
Tempusque Virgo p. 4
The Anatomy of Death p. 277

The ash and anguish of others grief (US) p. 246
The Baker p. 209
The Blessed Sacrament said here p. 12
The city darks, shadowed, lamp lit p. 300
The clean sky leaves undress the trees p. 26
The corn waits for its ripeness (S) p. 223
The Crone's Lament p. 61
The desert of your absence p. 273
The Dog p. 286
The earth's excited with leaf and labour p. 9
The Envoi p. 220
The Felucca is a slender-necked bird p. 288
The Fraser Canyon p. 179
The Geography of Women p. 153
The Gift p. 139
The girl at the factory took me in p. 30
The Horse p. 146
The Lake p. 169
The maddening traffic of my dreams p. 19
The Magnolia p. 345
The Mason's Epitaph p. 65
The Mill Leat p. 155
The Miller's Lament p. 42
The Mistress p. 140
The Mongrel p. 68
The Need p. 103
The Parting (LL) p. 265
The Philanderers' Lament p. 126
The notion held by scientists, philosophers and theologians p. 308
The Poet p. 221
The purpose of life is to increase awareness, sensitivity p. 179
The Quandary p. 290
The Reason p. 212
The reason I have not written (S) p. 306
The result of having p. 307
The revolving Earth p. 24
The Shell p. 255
The Single Eye p. 78
The Rose p. 308
The site: choose a dry site p. 82
The sky mooned with opals (LL) p. 264
The Survivors p. 162
The Thebans have conquered p. 289
The thick blood of my heart p. 84

The Thought p. 121
The tranquillity I find by this lake p. 169
The trouble from being as intelligent as I am p. 290
The U.S. Department of Justice considered (P) p. 196
The violet stars their petals fall (LL) p. 267
The West Ward holds six: (*The Ward*) p. 238
Their curiosity lacks concern p. 281
There have been many boats, many sailors before you p. 166
There have been many; only one (S) p. 99
There is a necessity for prayer (C) p. 318
There was a man who collected kindness p. 96
There was no part of you (S) p. 138
They are all either p. 290
They asked him: why all his songs were sad (LL) p. 261
They say I am a shit because I commit (US) p. 241
They say it is important to tell the truth (S) p. 252
They say that man is blessed with sight p. 78
They talk of love as if it were a thing (US) p. 248
They tell me it's my birthday. How old am I? p. 185
They tell you you're a pretty girl p. 153
This is spiritual vandalism p. 314
This rose weeps with its own petals (LL) p. 260
This song's to a girl p. 85
Thou, on a Cross; I, on a divided heart (S) p. 131
Thou, who grew so pure p. 97
Though earth lies heavy p. 206
Though I deny Time reality (S) p. 232
Though I do not know you personally p. 292
Thus weeps the rose and everything I see p. 225
To her whose eyes are eloquent since she p. 92
To The Bishop Of Coventry p. 154
To the lake of my aloneness (S) p. 105
To Plough p. 83
To-day an empty chair attacked me (LL) p. 257
To-day has been a sad day p. 272
Today, I am sad p. 134
Today the Vicar came down – it being Good Friday p. 31
Truth p. 257
Truth is derived from events p. 176
Two telegraph posts: no lines between them p. 270
Unfinished Eulogy p. 28
Unless I can forgive I shall corrode (US) p. 247
Value me no less (S) p. 342
Vancouver p. 186
Veins can, as vines climb, swell p. 33

Were the curls p. 20
What am I? This name p. 205
What a saboteur Time is p. 185
What can I do with my love (S) p. 127
What falls more lightly p. 152
What home's the swallow p. 223
What is it but hope (C) p. 325
What is love? p. 315
What is sex? p. 313
What is shame? p. 316
What is Summer? p. 57
What is this rose? p. 308
What lamb's as gentle? (S) p. 214
What love is this I feel for you p. 309
What seashell sleeves wave, surf or spray (S) p. 228
What's a woman but a funnel (US) p. 244
Wheels will wear acres in the ache of space p. 218
When all this place is rubble, ash and dross p. 140
When I asked Dr Hill (P) p. 193
When I peered into the bog of Irish history p. 177
When may I introduce to you p. 11
When men hunger and women p. 5
When Pound was in clink (P) p. 198
When we are young, old age is a period (C) p. 324
When you say you love me (P) p. 203
Where have her opal eyes flown? (S) p. 305
Where in this wide world can p. 146
Where quietness has roots; silence, leaves: p. 179
Where the earth floor was puddled with urine p. 151
Where the lyre to which these rows of vines p. 227
Where waves of earth p. 67
Where's the poem? (S) p. 98
Whether truth exists unless it is apprehended p. 257
White wings scissor the linen air; p. 273
Who are all those grey little men p. 184
Who Is The I? p. 319
Who is there who has not sometime, somewhere (US) p. 244
Who is this friend I can ignore p. 286
Who really loves me? p. 6
Who was it who nudged me when I sat lonely p. 309
Whose blood is this p. 101
Whose boots are these p. 162
Whose cruelty is this which now divides (S) p. 217
Why do I flee from you, since you pursue p. 284
Why do you laugh up Your sleeve of night (S) p. 104

Why do you run away and kneel p. 121
Why don't you ever write anything happy? she once asked (C) p. 327
Why is it when we ride together (S) p. 171
Wind Song p. 132
Winter ferrets knuckles of the banks (LL) p. 263
Winter, slippered with leaves p. 219
Winter's Song p. 301
With clouds as hands Death fingers pass p. 269
With silent wings (S) p. 344
With the vision of the blind p. 63
With vines entwined upon the trellis of her sleep p. 281
With what precipitous grave (LL) p. 261
Women p. 281
Words are a net (S) p. 130
Wound of earth bandaged by night (LL) p. 261
Yet would that these words could give (S) p. 189
You ask if I love you (P) p. 203
You ask me to write a poem (S) p. 137
You ask me where we came from? I will tell you p. 178
You ask me why I look so sad (P) p. 203
You ask the question p. 283
You claim you have given yourself to me (P) p. 204
You give yourself to me (P) p. 204
You have planted so many trees (S) p. 117
You say you love me (P) p. 203
You say you love me. Behind your eyes I see (P) 203
You say you love me and imply (P) p. 202
You stand upon the lip of an abyss p. 149
You think this makes us equal: nothing will (S) p. 122
You want to know what love is? (S) p. 304
Your cruelty was you were so kind (S) p. 316
Your death took everything from me (S) p. 172
Your from the depths: I, from the shallows (C) p. 339
Your leaving this morning (LL) p. 253
Your vagina is like a sea anemone (P) p. 204

| (C) | = Canto | (P) | = Paprika | (US) | = Unrhymed Sonnet |
| (LL) | = Last Lyric | (S) | = Solitude | | |